"What I'm about to say here will undoubtedly stir up considerable drama. So, the other important thing to remember is while it may SEEM or APPEAR there are 'good' and 'bad' aliens or humans for that matter, the Universe at its core has good intentions although life/consciousness may get confused at times in its means of achieving those always positive goals.

A perfect example being the cover up of the UFO phenomenon – the aim was to keep humans 'free' of outside influence. But 'hiding' things or abilities was not the right approach. If the goal is freedom or freedom of expression, the steps along the way should reflect the sought after freedom and include the free exchange of information and ideas."

-   From *Fire Sight: True Stories of Miracles & Immortality*

I0167098

Other work by Jason Nealon:

Website: http://www.firesnakeprophecy.com

Twitter: https://twitter.com/ProphecySnake

YouTube: www.youtube.com/c/Firesnakeprophecy

FIRE SNAKE PROPHECY

FIRE
SIGHT

TRUE STORIES OF MIRACLES & IMMORTALITY

JASON NEALON, M.D.

FIRE SNAKE PROPHECY. FIRE SIGHT: TRUE
STORIES OF MIRACLES & IMMORTALITY

Front Cover Art: DVARG
Back Cover Art: Graphic Compressor

Published by Fire Snake Prophecy
http://www.firesnakeprophecy.com

ISBN-13:978-0-9987530-0-3

CONTENTS

SECTION 2: TRANSCRIPTS FROM PODCASTS/VIDEOCASTS

SECTION 3: BOOK CHAPTER

To all the mythical Centaurs who helped raise me.

"Witness me." - Mad Max: Fury Road

INTRODUCTORY NOTES

You may have already figured out this book is not like any others. And I'm actually happy with that. Because I think it reflects the true nature of reality better than trying to fit things into prescribed categories.

That wasn't the original plan for this book. And the plans have changed so many times I don't know if they could be called plans anymore. There seems to be an energy that wants to express itself, and at times it feels like I'm just along for the ride.

And that ride doesn't always follow linear time. Which tends to upset a great majority of people.

So, while I can't say for certain what will happen tomorrow. What I do have today is this collection of work for your consideration.

I don't think the material needs a lengthy introduction as they were created as stand-alone pieces to begin with.

There are a couple of things I would like to draw attention to since all of this material has been converted from different source material.

I feel some of the blog posts gain a new dimension when read on my website due to being able to link to different sources on the internet: (http://www.firesnakeprophecy.com).

The transcriptions of the Podcasts/Videocasts I think hold up very well on their own. Obviously, I would recommend taking the time to watch or listen if possible though.

Stealing Fire was Chapter 1 of the book I sent to agents and publishers. Some may feel the material is repetitive of the 1st Videocast. However, I believe the written format of a book allows for expression in ways not achievable with other technologies.

So, without further ado…

More Than You Ever Wanted to Know About Aliens – Part 1

By Fire Snake| January 20th, 2017|Categories: Aliens, UFOs|Tags: Digestive System

This was originally from a discussion on the Reddit forums. It received a good response there, so I wanted to make it available here as well. Here is the actual thread.

People were asking for more threads on aliens in this forum the other day. I had written some stuff a while back and just added some more to it recently.

The title of the original thread was: Why Do Aliens Look Humanoid?

"I will try to answer this question. You have to keep in mind this is from a reliable source, but it is second hand information – so there will always be some distortion regardless of efforts to the contrary.

What I'm about to say here will also undoubtedly stir up considerable drama. So, the other important thing to remember is while it may SEEM or APPEAR there are 'good' and 'bad' aliens or humans for that matter, the universe at its core has good intentions although life/consciousness may get confused at times in its means of achieving those always positive goals.

A perfect example being the cover up of the UFO phenomenon – the aim was to keep humans 'free' of outside influence, but 'hiding' things or abilities was not the right approach. If the goal is freedom or freedom of expression, the steps along the way should reflect the sought after freedom and include the free exchange of information and ideas.

The first thing you might want to check out is the Tom Delonge interview on Coast to Coast if you haven't already. Pay particular attention to the 4th hour from 12:30-13:30.

What is important here is not just what is said, but also what is not said. Delonge brings up the connections with gravity and consciousness, and then the host George Knapp says:

"There is high level interest in that area and some of the brightest minds are working on it".

The question you should be asking at this point is, "Who are these bright minds working at a high level on this problem?" And here is where the information from my source comes into play.

At this point, I'm going to need to refer you to a thread on ATS about a Nostradamus prophecy about a Great Genius. Here and Here. Now, what my source tells me is that this guy exists. Right now. And this is exactly one of the problems he is working on – gravity and consciousness. The reason no one knows about him should be obvious. The truth behind gravity would shatter the scientific world and the truth about consciousness would shatter the religious world.

And apparently this guy's real identity is so guarded he doesn't even work in a top secret or classified government lab. He literally lives like a yeti or sasquatch out in the wilderness studying nature. And when the government wants information from him they have to trek out into the woods and dodge UFO's a la the story from Ingo Swann's book 'Penetration'.

I can't vouch for the rest of the Nostradamus prophecies, especially the end of the world destruction stuff, and I think Nostradamus himself was quick to point out that a lot of that stuff could be avoided if we tried hard enough – this was his whole reason for making the prophecies was so they COULD be avoided. But he also said this Great Genius guy was just an unavoidable 'nexus point' in our time-frame.

What does this have to do with aliens looking like humans you say? Well, it's absolutely essential to understand consciousness if we want to understand aliens. The second thing to check out was also recently mentioned again by Delonge in his ATS AMA and this is the Corso book and diary – 'The Day After Roswell '. This is from chapter 7 talking about the EBE (Extra Terrestrial Biological Entity):

"And if an exchange of nutrients and waste occurred within their systems, that exchange could have only taken place through the creature's skin or the outer protective covering they wore because there were no digestive or waste systems".

So, there's no digestive system. They have all the other organ systems – heart, brain, lungs, skin, bones, blood, muscles, but no digestive system. Why? What is unique about the human digestive system? And here is where gravity and consciousness come into play. The center of gravity in humans is located in the gut. The center of gravity in relation to what? The EARTH.

If the aliens took some humans or some humans volunteered to go with them and left earth's gravity – their center of gravity would obviously change. This is why when you see reports sometimes of people saying the aliens wobbled, or jumped or floated or had on strange shoes is because they have no EARTH center of gravity. But they do still have CONSCIOUSNESS.

Well, why and how does that happen? We have to go back again to the Great Genius prophecies again where they say he will "duplicate or transfer his genius into an organic computer".

Corso also talks about the EBE as being some kind of robot or drone – but made out of organic tissue. A kind of 'organic computer'. If a human genius can put his consciousness into another 'container', then it would be no sweat for an alien intelligence to transfer its consciousness into a human vessel. They already do it on EARTH when people "channel" entities that come through and control their vocal chords.

If they did it in SPACE where the gravity was different and they had a closet full of human suits who volunteered to help them then the human suits would change over time to adapt to the new environment and the center of gravity would no longer be in the stomach – no more digestive system needed.

OK. What about the outward physical appearance apart from the organ systems? Do these 'humanoid' aliens at all resemble a computer? They have no ears, no mouth, no nose – but huge eyes. How do we get information from our current computers? A huge display right? Eyes = Monitor – the biggest part of a computer.

Our computers don't "feed" us information into our mouths = no mouth needed. Our computers don't generate "smells" = no nose needed. Our computers don't "speak" a verbal language to us = no ears needed. They use VISUAL images – the universal language of symbols – again the need for huge eyes, but no other sense organs. Our computers are a primitive form of visual/emotional mental telepathy.

The last thing that is worth looking into is a book called "Revelation: The Divine Fire" by Brad Steiger. On page 217 of that book the author is quoting the 'Seth Material' talking about our future when he says:

"Man's experience will be so extended, that to you the race will seem to have changed into another. This does not mean there will not be problems. It does mean that man will have far greater resources at his command. It also presupposes a richer and far more diverse social framework…"

Again, what is being said here without being said? Man will be almost unrecognizable = alien. Far greater resources = alien technology. More diverse social framework = intergalactic alien brotherhood.

And as far as the time travel stuff. The Seth Material does the best job I've seen of explaining 'simultaneous time' and how time really works and that this stuff – the past/present/future – is all happening at once. We will be alien/We will be us – all at the same time.

Lastly, this is not even the tip of the iceberg. The "grays" that this explanation was given to me about are not even close to the only consciousness that we interact with."

More Than You Ever Wanted to Know About Aliens – Part 2

By Fire Snake| January 20th, 2017|Categories: Aliens, UFOs|Tags: Neurological System

And here's some of the new thoughts regarding the neurological system:

One of the other interesting and stand out things Corso talked about with the EBE was that while the autopsy reported there was a nervous system – it was different than ours in that the brain had 4 lobes instead of 2 hemispheres (the circulatory system was also slightly different in using lymphatic fluid instead of blood, and I'm going to need a separate post to address that aspect).

But as far as the brain goes, what do they need 4 lobes for? Well, in order to understand what the extra lobes are for, you need to understand what our 2 lobes do first. Basically, one lobe represents the "past" and one lobe represents the "future" – and when they work together you get a sum that's greater than the parts and they produce what we consider the "present". Seth again hints at this in 'The Unknown Reality Vol 1' pages 97-99:

"Basically, the cell's comprehension straddles time as you think of it. Hunters had to respond at once to the present situation. The cell's basic innocence of time discrimination had to be bypassed. At deeply unconscious levels the neurological structure is more highly adaptable than it appears. Adjustments were made, therefore. Basically, the neurological structure responds to both past and future data."

So, he's saying we started with a 1 lobe brain. But the "past" kept interfering with the "present" and people were responding to things from the past that weren't really there (a big problem when trying to track down food) and the brain had to "split" into 2 lobes in order to alleviate this problem.

And so if the brain hemispheres split once – it can split again – like a developing zygote or embryo 1,2,4,8, etc. What exactly do these 2 extra lobes do for the "aliens" (or us if you want to look at it that way)? I'm not sure entirely. If I had to guess, I would probably start with the behavior and then work backwards to the function.

What can aliens do that we can't? Telepathy, anti-gravity, traveling "through" space. These are all manipulations of "space" in a way. Somehow "time" has disappeared for them.

So, it appears these two extra lobes are related to "time". Well, if the two lobes we already have deal with aspects of time (past and future) it wouldn't be a stretch to assume the two new lobes also deal with time – possibly "slow" and "fast" manipulations – since Seth also talks about how there are nerve impulses that leap too slowly or too quickly for the synapses.

Slow and fast functions would also help to explain other behavior of UFO's with the incredible speeds reported or the strange behavior of the 'falling leaf motion' when coming in for a landing. (If these craft are indeed controlled by 'thought' then what does a thought look like? – Similarities between brainwave tracing turned sideways and the falling leaf pattern. Also, when "time" disappears like it does for the aliens you also get immortality.

Another interesting aspect is Seth's mention of "ghost images" of future probabilities. Is he referring to UFO's? Are these ghost images the lobe of the brain dealing with the "future" overpowering the lobe that deals with the "past"? It would to help explain why UFO's seem to change with the time period.

Oh yeah – Going back the digestive system or gut that's missing in the aliens. This also helps explain some of the weird behavior of the Men in Black.

Like the story where the guy was in a diner and ordered a steak and didn't know how to eat it. Or the other story about the guy trying to drink Jell-O like it was soup. And not MiB, but the 'space pancake' story also deals with food.

Another weird thing the aliens do besides wobble around because they have no center of gravity and playing with their food. They also have a fascination with asking people, "What time is it?" Are they really asking a question or telling us the future – one where time disappears and we join them/us in immortality?

Edit 1: Also related to the food – Ingo Swann's encounter with the alien near LA was at a supermarket.

Edit 2: I think the food is symbolism like the statement they make about "What time is it?". They're not asking – they're telling (fortune telling) – and with the food they're saying something about how we use energy.

Edit 3: Again with the food symbolism. This could also explain the mutilated cattle. Like they're trying to understand why we would use that as an energy source. Also the anal probing. They totally don't understand how we use energy – the intake or the output – it's like it confuses them (us?)

Edit 4: The 4 lobes of the brain – is this what Leonardo da Vinci saw when he sketched the helicopter with 4 blades? (He supposedly had an ET encounter in a cave when he was younger). And when the blades spin around that's similar to how our energy spirals in our body? Golden spirals everywhere here too.

More Than You Ever Wanted to Know About Aliens – Part 3

By Fire Snake| January 20th, 2017|Categories: Aliens, UFOs|Tags: Lymphatic System

This is the update to include a short discussion of the lymphatic system:

OK. I mentioned I was going to need a separate post for this. I wasn't planning on making that post for a little while because I haven't completely gathered my thoughts on it yet, but I'll outline what I have so far like I did with the gut and brain and maybe we can figure it out together.

This is what Corso says about the circulation of the EBE in Chapter 7 of "The Day After Roswell" page 49:

"Of specific interest was the fluid that served as blood but also seemed to regulate bodily functions in much the same way glandular secretions do for the human body. In these biological entities, the blood system and lymphatic systems seem to have been combined."

So, here's where I started to try to figure this out. With the gut, I asked myself, "What's unique about the gut and why wouldn't aliens have one?".

And that's how I made the connection between it being the center of gravity. Aliens do weird things with gravity and they don't have digestion – and flip flopped – we can't do weird things with gravity yet and we do have a digestive system. More golden spirals if you like that angle (I also have some more material on the inner ear I'd like to get into in another post).

Anyways, the immune system is a highly complicated system that is a major topic of study not just in medical science, but among the general public as well with the discussions of vaccines, germs, etc. So, if we ask the same question again, "What's unique about the lymphatic system and why do the aliens favor that instead of blood like we use?" It brought me back to gravity again.

The lymph works only in one direction and it is against gravity. Both the immunological function of the lymph and the actual lymphogenic process are not clearly understood even today. The subject of the lymph is complex and very much unsettled.

Well, OK. The lymph is working against gravity. And so are the aliens with their anti-gravity tech so it makes sense they would have more lymph than blood.

What's also interesting is – In contrast to mammalian erythrocytes (Red Blood Cells – RBC's), which have lost their nucleus and mitochondria during maturation, the erythrocytes of almost all other vertebrate species are nucleated throughout their lifespan.

So, taking those statements into account, it seems we are on track to become 'aliens' before the other vertebrate species who still have nucleated RBC's – our circulation appears to be more "evolved" or "advanced" comparatively. Blood is getting phased out and replaced with lymph. Basically, there's some big changes going on.

And what happens when things change a lot is often there are 'side effects' or 'problems'. So, our brains are going through some big changes – and if you look around everyone is complaining that everyone else has lost their 'mind'. There's also a lot of new and weird neurological phenomenon's which you would expect when a mind is expanding and causing the brain to expand in turn.

That's also another area where people are complaining really hard about 'side effects' or 'problems' – the whole issues surrounding vaccines and immune functions. It would also make sense, like with the expanding brain, that if our circulatory/lymphatic system was changing significantly – we would also expect some significant immunological problems along the way.

This is pretty long already so I'll just throw some seasoning on top here of a few other things I think are related, but haven't organized into a comprehensive whole yet.

One way to look at our interactions with aliens and their technology would be similar to how we describe immune reactions in our bodies. We've been vaccinated with alien technology (computer chips/night vison/lasers/fiber optics), but not immune to the aliens themselves. Socially, their (our future?) existence makes a lot of people feel sick or ill.

Lastly, I have some vague ideas about bird migration and electromagnetic energy and how consciousness interacts with these and it may have something to do with everything mentioned above. Here's an article, but like I said I don't know what to make of it quite yet talking about – the bony fish, amphibians, reptiles, and birds, having true lymphatic vascular systems, but cartilaginous fish do not have a true lymph system.

Also, going all the way back to talking about the gut. The pineal gland is not actually a part of the brain, rather it develops from specialized tissues in the roof of the fetal mouth – and the mouth is the beginning of the GI tract.

Edit 1: I'm sure some people have already decided I've gone completely "off the rails" (as if there are any 'rails' anyways). So, I'll go ahead and push it even further since I've already gotten into cell biology and nucleation – eukaryotic cell nucleus the original crop circle?

Edit 2: Also interesting, if you want to continue the food symbolism, that the current crop circles are being created right in the middle of food/energy sources. I think they're (we?) are really trying to give us a message.

Edit 3: One note I forgot about – The presence of cerebrospinal fluid (CSF) in the lymphatic system and the presence of neurotransmitter receptors on immune cells, suggests a powerful association between neurotransmitters and immune function.

Edit 4: It's going to take a while for me to get the inner ear information together, there's just a whole lot of stuff. But I will say now, there's also a connection with lymphatics because the inner ear uses a fluid called endolymph. Meniere's disease is also highly interesting if people want to look into stuff on their own.

Past Life Regression to Contact Paul the Apostle – Kickstarter

By Fire Snake| January 21st, 2017|Categories: Philosophy, Religion|Tags: Paul the Apostle

This was the first Kickstarter I attempted to get funding for. The goal wasn't reached, but it can always be resubmitted. So, if anyone is interested in getting this off the ground, the option is still there.

About this project

I realize this is a bit of a strange project to request funding for. So, of course naturally there's a bit of a strange story behind the request.

One night I was at a bar having a pint with a friend (it always starts this way right?). Anyhow, the conversation came around to Terence McKenna and UFOs. And towards the end of our discussion I brought forth my theory that McKenna could possibly be the reincarnation of John the Baptist. Not just the similarities in the work they did throughout their lives, but also in physical resemblance.

Now, I thought I had taken it "far out there" when I said that, but my friend then comes back at me with, "Well, you know what? Your life resembles St. Paul's a lot and even your looks do too."

I won't get into it too much here, but a few years ago I had a near death experience, which kind of changed everything in my life. Not long before that happened, I also had a strange thing happen when my lifelong myopic vision suddenly healed or cured itself. So, he was referring to when Paul had his experience on the road to Damascus. If you ask me, I don't know. It's possible.

Anyway, that's the background. On to the project. So, most people would leave this as bar room banter. Maybe brought up again, or maybe too weird and never talked about again. The problem with my theory of McKenna/John the Baptist is of course neither one is still living. If McKenna was still alive, we could have asked him to do a past life regression through hypnosis. He was game for a lot of fringe experimentation with the mind. It's possible he would have agreed.

Well, I'm still alive though. So, we can test my friend's crazy theory of me and Paul the Apostle. And so that's what this little project is about. I've looked into it and the total cost to do this would be $585. I will put the line item breakdown below.

The hypnotist was chosen because he's trained with Brian Weiss, the author of the bestseller "Many Lives, Many Masters ". Brain Weiss is a professor of Psychiatry at the University of Miami School of Medicine (which is also where I went school).

And the hypnotist's office is only 4 hours away from my home in Tampa. So, this could possibly be done in one day – although I've budgeted for overnight.

$350 Past Life Hypnosis
$100 Hotel
$75 Gas
$60 Fees
$585 Total

So, this is just small little project right now. It may become something bigger – or it may be a dud. For such a small investment though – it seems worth pursuing. The hypnotist I chose is also comfortable with being video recorded and makes tapes for all his sessions.

The movie from the session is what the documentary will consist of. It's hard to say in advance how long this recording will be. And if something interesting does turn up under hypnosis it could turn into a longer story and documentary, which would then require a re-submission for further funding.

Risks and challenges

I'm on the West Coast right now, but I plan to be in Florida by December. I've already talked to the hypnotist about scheduling an appointment during that time and he said it should be no problem.

Additional Resources

If any of what I've brought up sounds interesting to anyone, there's some additional aspects to this whole experiment that could come into play and may help shed further light on whatever comes up in the hypnosis session. The Seth Material, for those not familiar, talks a good bit about the historical Christ entity and also what to expect when he returns.

Seth claimed to have an entire book ready to be dictated on Christ if that was what the channelers, Jane and Robert Butts, desired. As far as I'm aware, they never took him up on this offer. And related to that, I may look into putting together another Kickstarter to fund a trip to the Yale Library to look through all the unpublished material and research for myself and others (I think there's 498 boxes of material).

Links

The original Kickstarter funding page can be viewed here. Some of Terence McKenna's most popular books: Food of the Gods, True Hallucinations and The Archaic Revival. A couple of Seth's most popular books: Seth Speaks and The Nature of Personal Reality.

A Modern Take On Jung's Psychosis Experiments – Kickstarter

By Fire Snake| January 21st, 2017|Categories: Meditation, Psychology|Tags: Carl Jung

In case you're not familiar, this article summarizes it well:

"Jung reportedly found a way to bring on his unconscious stream of thoughts and visions at will — something most people today who experience psychosis or schizophrenia can't do. Nor can they do the opposite — make them go away by just willing it."

So, I just did a new podcast the other day talking about how I healed my lifelong myopic vision. I was satisfied with the explanation I gave, but couldn't help thinking there was more to it than I was grasping at the moment.

The way I described it was along the lines of – I was already making several really big changes in my life – so thinking I could do without my glasses didn't seem that 'far out' there among all the other big new things that were happening. Basically, changes attract other changes and it's easier to make big changes when you're already making big changes.

And so I started playing around with this concept some more and it lead me to: If you want big changes at the end, you need to make big changes in order to get there. And when you boil it down even further – what we're looking to do is make big changes to our minds because big changes in the physical world follow automatically once you've made big changes to the mind.

So, if you wanted to make yourself into a super genius – small incrementally studying along the way won't cut it. If you want drastic changes to your mind at the end, you're going to have to do some drastic things to your mind along the way. So, with my eyes, I made some fairly decent size changes to my mind, and saw some fairly decent size changes in my visual acuity.

I'm wondering if you could even take this a step further. I've already changed my body by changing my mind. Is it possible to direct evolution and make such drastic changes to the mind – that the structure of the brain changes so much as to open up entirely new physical abilities?

I know this is how it works for sure too because this is also how I induced a near death experience. I made such drastic changes to my mind in my visualizations that I ended up with a very dramatic change in my mind at the end with a NDE – and also changes in the physical world as a result of how much my mind had changed by occupying two bodies at once.

And another word for drastic changes to the mind is imagination.

Imagination is the action of forming new ideas, or images or concepts.

So, if you're looking to form new ideas – you're going to need to look at the problem from a different perspective. In Jung's case – his different perspective was intentional psychosis. Mathematicians also use intentional psychosis to get a different perspective (but use amphetamines to get there). Rich people use money instead of amphetamines as a way to "detach themselves from reality" and get a different perspective in order to form new ideas.

The goal of all these people (whether the esoteric use of will by Jung, drugs by academics, or money by business people) the goal is all the same – to obtain a different perspective in order to increase imagination and generation of ideas and ultimately dramatic changes to the mind that will manifest in the 3D physical world.

That was a long way to go, but what I'm wanting to do is a Kickstarter aimed at helping me bring on a psychosis.

I'm thinking the most socially acceptable way to do it is how the business community does it – with money. So, I was thinking if I raised enough money to go 'crazy' for a week or two and filmed the whole thing it would almost be an update or sequel to the Red Book by Jung – because I feel I can also "control" the onset and remission of the psychotic state like he did.

Related Thoughts

Some of the other interesting things that came up while thinking about this is – why are people always trying to find a different perspective? Could it be that unbridled imagination (psychosis) is the default state that gets "learned" out of us as we grow up? Are we just trying to reconnect with our natural existence?

And this also ties in with some thoughts I was having about immortality. So, if you want immortality at the end, you're going to need to use immortality to get there. How in the heck do you do that though? Well, the spirit is immortal, yeah? So, you've got to use the spirit. And immortality means without "time". So, add it up – and you need to "use the spirit outside of time" if you want immortality at the end.

OK. Well, that just opens up more questions. How do you use the spirit outside of time? I think I did this with my NDE and eyesight healing.

I'm also thinking sex and music are other ways to use the spirit outside of time. I bet if you asked someone in the middle of having sex what time they thought it was – they wouldn't be very accurate. Just like there is no time in dreams. Music is also a very easy way to time travel – why people have a fondness for music from their youth.

Is that what inducing psychosis is? Using the spirit outside of time? Immortality?

Summary

I like the approach I've outlined above for several reasons.

Right off the bat, Jung has been accepted into mainstream culture. So, by structuring this experiment around work that already owns widespread "mental real estate" in public consciousness makes the explaining I have to do much, much less.

Secondly, by declaring beforehand my intention is to go crazy, there should be no confusion when things get real weird. Related to this – if the project did get funding – no one could accuse me of trying to "force" my beliefs or views on anyone.

Because people voted with their wallets – this is what they wanted to see – this is what they summoned into reality. There would be no one single person responsible or the target of criticism since this is what the public literally asked for.

And lastly before this gets too long, I think the 'means' being used here are a very good reflection of the 'ends' I'm looking to reach. I'd like to see this stuff talked about publicly – OK, well let's get the public involved from the beginning. I'd also like to see more transparency – so I have no problem opening up every little nook and cranny of my psyche for people to have a look for themselves.

Additional Resources

Links to some of Carl Jung's more accessible books: Man and His Symbols, The Undiscovered Self, Memories, Dreams, Reflections. Amphetamine use among high level mathematicians and academics – Paul Erdos, Anthony Hopkins in the movie Proof, Adderall, Ritalin, and Vyvanse use at colleges and universities.

Time-Table for The Return of Christ

By Fire Snake| January 21st, 2017|Categories: Philosophy, Religion|Tags: Return of Christ

This was another discussion that originally took place on Reddit I wanted to share here.

The "Law of One" material was the topic of conversation and here is the context of my comments and this is a link to the complete thread.

I agree Wilcock does have a ton of interesting material. Personally, I found his discussion of how objects get embedded inside other objects during tornadoes fascinating – I don't remember his exact explanation of the mechanism – but really interesting. (I have some of my own thoughts on this phenomenon as well)

But there's something about the "Law of One" material I can't put my finger on. One of my thoughts for why I get a vagueness from it is that it's possible the whole thing was created by the CIA to discount all the other people who were doing channeling around that time like Jane Roberts and Seth and others like the Council of Nine, Spectra, Scientology, etc.

The specific reason why I doubt the "Law of One" material is because it's the only source I've heard say that Christ isn't going to return. Seth says Christ is coming back. Edgar Cayce says Christ is coming back (although Cayce sometimes interpreted the Second Coming of Christ as being an internal, psychic event within the individual seeker, and sometimes as the actual return of Jesus Christ).

Nostradamus talks about a "Great Genius" who he says some people will interpret as a Second Coming. Even the Spectra intelligence that Uri Geller was associated with remarked there would be another person in 50 years' time (50 years from 1970 so around 2020). And obviously Christ himself in the bible talks about his return.

It seems most of the top tier channeling material all say there will be some advanced "being" or "entity" coming around soon except the "Law of One". (The dates all slightly vary. Seth said 1975-2075. Cayce gave a date around 1998. Spectra was also in that ballpark – 2020). Nostradamus also said around now. Why is the "Law of One" the only one saying Christ isn't coming back?

Who would have to something to gain from keeping humanity depressed and keeping them from Christ? The CIA and the Cabal/Shadow Government have a history of wanting to stop the people getting all excited about anything. Curbing enthusiasm. Easier to control sluggish population. (War of the Worlds/Orson Welles)
Here's the exact wording the "Law of One" uses when talking about a return of Christ:

"I will attempt to sort out this question. It is difficult…The particular mind/body/spirit complex you call Jesus is, as what you would call an entity, not to return except as a member of the Confederation occasionally speaking through a channel."

So, I guess this gets really complicated if you take into account what Seth says about Christ the last time he was here being John the Baptist, Jesus, and Paul all at the same time.

So, if those were just different personalities all from the same entity, then if the "entity" comes back – you could technically say it wouldn't be Jesus but a "new" personality – and it might even be possible to contact the Jesus personality through regression hypnosis of whatever "new personality" he comes back as – and this is the "channeling" that Ra is talking about above?

Looking at it that way – I guess the "Law of One" Ra material could be right. "Jesus" specifically won't be back. But a different personality of Jesus. And maybe that's why Ra also says "It is difficult" – difficult to explain in a way that makes sense? And this could be why Cayce also appeared to say contradictory statements about it being – an internal psychic event, but also as an actual return (maybe Cayce is also referring to the contacting Jesus through hypnosis when he says "internal psychic event"?)

That got longer than I anticipated. Anyways, the last thing I wanted to say is that it could possibly just be an issue I'm personally having right now – and the reason the "Law of One" comes across as vague to me right now is that it's highly advanced material and I'm not ready for it yet and that's why I'm having a hard time understanding. Who knows.

A Little More

I forgot to add another reason why the "Law of One" doesn't sit right with me. I guess compared to something like the Seth Material, when I hear people talk about their experiences with Seth – they're almost always saying the information and knowledge immediately improved their life in a practical day to day existence. The thing is – I hardly ever hear about people discussing the Seth Material (nowadays) – it's almost like it's being, not totally suppressed, but maybe a little suppression, or not a lot of active fans.

On the other hand, fans of the "Law of One" seem to be inordinately vocal about how great the material is. Yet, never from a single admirer have I heard a person say how it improved their day to day existence in an immediate, practical, easy to understand way like people report with the Seth Material. Like I said, I don't know why this is, but it seems strange to me. And when strange is around the CIA is not far behind.

Also, let's look at how the "Law of One" is presented, or dare I say intentionally constructed by an intelligence agency. Right off the bat, the thing is nearly unreadable. It's almost as if it was designed for people to take a quick look and then dismiss anything having to do with channeling because it's almost incomprehensible.

Then you also have the similarities with Seth, and Ra both being Egyptian Deities. "Law of One" came out shortly after Seth – similar time periods. It's almost like they wanted these two books to appear nearly identical. One seeming to be full of gibberish though and the other elegant and coherent and practical.

This seems to me almost transparent as intentionally created disinformation. (There's also the similarities in both the Seth and Ra channeling having multiple volumes of work) I also don't want to implicate David Wilcock in anything, but if he was roommates with the "Law of One" author – I mean this is also textbook intelligence operative embedding themselves in the psychic community.

It's hard to believe that's even a job – disinformation agent – but it is – and the government employs tons of them. What's even harder to believe is that someone sees that job listing – go confuse people – and decide that's something that's worth their time. Amazing really.
Lastly, one of Ra's big things or teachings is the concept of 'service to self or service to others'. What I don't understand is why people think these are two separate things?

From my experience in the world, it's entirely possible to find something that you selfishly love to do, but also at the same time benefits and serves everyone else as much as you. It's just confusing to me that people can't accept that a thing can fall into more than more category or be more than one thing at a time. Something can benefit/fulfill you while at the same time benefiting and fulfilling everyone else.

And I think this is what Aleister Crowley was getting at with True Will. Sure, there are a lot of things we selfishly like to do. This could be seen as will with a little 'w'. But when you hold these little wills up for everyone to take a look – they get a big thumbs down. Other people don't appreciate them as much as you.

True Will on the other hand is "True" because it selfishly satisfies you – but then when you hold it up for others to examine – you get a big thumbs up this time and everyone else appreciates it as much as you. Now your 'will' has passed the 'true test' and becomes "True Will".

I want to mention or point out again. These are just my current thoughts at the moment. I could be very wrong. My reason for sharing these ideas is I feel they may be helpful to people in the current moment even if some of my observations and speculations turn out to be off the mark.

Additional Resources

Edgar Cayce – The Sleeping Prophet, Reading 2067-7 concerning Jesus ministry, Seth excerpts about Cayce and Pyramid Gestalt Personalities. Conversations with Nostradamus. Seth Speaks.

Religion A Reflection of Consciousness

By Fire Snake| January 23rd, 2017|Categories:
Consciousness, Religion|Tags: Religion Reflecting
Consciousness

I like the statement by Seth/Jane Roberts that Religion
is always a reflection of the Consciousness of
whatever time period or era.

There's a lot of reasons I like Seth. And actually, going
back through my notes last night I found something
he said which sounds like the double negative theory I
was playing with the other day:

"The problems begin when the field of available
choices is limited. This curtails the range of
expression. The individual then begins a concentrated
effort to seek out those avenues of expression still
open." (He was talking about how fanatics are
created. They all start off as idealists and then
frustration mounts. My notes are a mess though right
now and I can't find where he originally said this).

But back to Religion being a reflection of Consciousness. If this is true (which I think it is), you could even draw conclusions (make predictions) about what our next Religion will look like based upon what our consciousness is currently focused on.

Right now we love money, technology, altered states, mental superpowers, other dimensions, aliens even. And if you look at the most recent fairly popular Religion – Scientology – they check off a lot or all of those boxes.

Back in Biblical times though, it gets really difficult to imagine what their consciousness was like. Putting yourself in someone's shoes from 100 years ago is mind blowing, multiply that by a factor of 20 and it can get wild. It seems they were highly interested in peace, which is why they had Jesus or the Prince of Peace. He was supposed to be the first King that was not a 'War'rior King.

Seth also says in the ancient past consciousness was much more mobile. If someone wanted to experience what is was like to be a waterfall or butterfly, they could just transfer their mind into those things and have that experience.

So, it seems fairly obvious our conscious minds have changed over the years if you look at how Religion has changed over the corresponding time frame. The interesting part, to me at least, is not whether our minds our indeed changing – but what exactly are the changes that took place and is it possible to see where we might be headed?

This might not be the best analogy, but I think a lot of people have played video games before so I guess I'll use it. So, a couple thousand years ago the image of God was kind of an angry guy. It seems there was a lot of frustration or disappointment that was going on the conscious minds of that period.

Similar to how when you get a new video game (new features of consciousness), there's a learning curve and a lot of times the developers of the game will include a few easier "training" missions to get you used to the controls that are probably different than the last game you played. Well, real life doesn't have "training" missions. You give birth to a child (or new aspect of consciousness) and you are 100% parent now – kind of like how you can't be a little pregnant.

And as time went on people got better at the video game (and being parents of a new kind of consciousness), and got used to the new controls. Now they start saying things like "God is dead" because they're doing fine in their game and so the image of God that is reflected in Religion kind of disappears (Hey we got Science who needs God!).

And so these people keep playing the game. They get better and better at it, and their confidence is building and building. Now when the concept of God is brought up, they say "I'm a God!", "Can't you see all the great things I'm doing in my game?" – and enter our current Religion of Narcissism – a reflection of our conscious minds right now.

However, as anyone who's played a video game before knows. There's always comes a "Boss Battle". And usually for the most dramatic impact there's also a "calm before the storm" where the tension builds for the greatest contrast. I think that's where we are right now.

I want to emphasize though, this "Boss Battle" is nothing exterior that is being thrust upon anyone from the outside. It's a battle of the conscious mind to give birth to something new from the interior. Of course there will be effects in the 3D world, because that's why we're here. But if you want to look at it in cause and effect terms like science does, the source or cause is coming from within.

Also, this "birth" of a new consciousness is hard to accept for many. Especially the narcissistic parents. Some of them would like to murder the child before it's even formed. Again, going back to video games. These narcissistic parents are like the high score record holders on an old game like "Galaga".

The child wants to play a new game, but the narcissistic parents want to force the child to play the "old game" so they and their "records" aren't forgotten. All mandalas are made to be washed away though. The sooner the narcissists realize this, the less traumatic the birthing process will be.

Taking all this into consideration brings up some interesting things to speculate about.

Why the need to feel so sure or confident in ourselves (even overconfident/narcissistic)? Is the challenge we are coming up against equal in magnitude to the amount of narcissism we are witnessing?

Has Politics replaced Religion as the focus of our concentration and the place where we direct all our energy and "prayers"? And if that's the case, can we look at our most recently elected President and see any parallels with Religion?

President Trump has a fondness for money, real estate, celebrities, and overthrowing governments (Drain The Swamp). These values appear to line up extremely well with the previously mentioned interests of our most recent fairly popular religion – Scientology (Drain The Swamp – Operation Snow White).

Sports, Magic & The Zone (or Flow State)

By Fire Snake| January 23rd, 2017|Categories: Meditation, Sports|Tags: Golf and Flow

This blog post is a combination of an ad for golf lessons I originally posted on Craigslist and some thoughts about entering "the zone" for optimal athletic performance from a discussion on Reddit.

I know. You're looking at that picture and wondering if it's some kind of illusion right? How is that possible? How did he do that to that poor little golf club?

The answer is – magic is real. What you're seeing there is called "lag" in golf lingo. Lag just means "storing of energy". Maybe you've heard stories of Tai Chi masters who can "store energy" or "compact energy" into their bones and increase or decrease their physical weight at will?

Well, that's what I've done to that poor little golf club. I've just "stored" or "compacted" a ridiculous amount of energy into the atoms and molecules and matter that make up that driver.

The magic trick doesn't end there either.

The real art is in transferring that stored energy into the ball in an *extremely precise* manner. I don't want to get too much into quantum physics, but there's a principle that states you can't know the exact location and speed of a particle.

You can know either one with certainty, but not -both- the 'location' and 'speed'. This is what the game of golf is all about – getting as close as possible to knowing with certainty these two variables. Golfers call them "power" and "precision". Most people have one or the other – just like quantum physics 'location' or 'speed'. To have both in a single person is the Holy Grail and what produces all-time great champions such as Jack Nicklaus or Tiger Woods.

I mean, think about it – you have a ball you want to go far and ALSO to a precise spot. It needs "power" (velocity) and "precision" (location). Yes, in short I've defied the laws of physics. This is what magicians do. This is what magic is. It only becomes science when it's explained. Which I can explain to you for the low low price of…see rates at the end.

If you doubt my abilities or my status as a Wizard, my accomplishments range far beyond the field of golf. In fact – if I bothered to apply for Sainthood – I would most likely be a shoe in – since my miracles performed count is already at 2-3 depending on who you ask.

My first miracle was curing my lifelong myopic vision with only the power of my thoughts. My second miracle was inducing a near death experience with just the use of my mind. The 3rd miracle has yet to be brought into physical reality because of concerns about "necromancy" (which it most definitely is not – here's the Kickstarter project if you want to read about it yourself)

And if you doubt magic is real in general, then why do you think they refer to Phil Jackson as the "Zen Master"? Why all the Spiritual books about Athletes and Sports such as "The Way of the Peaceful Warrior" or "Golf in the Kingdom" or even "The Karate Kid"? Magic may be *denied* as existing, but that does not mean it doesn't exist – only that *denial* exists.

I can be your Mr. Miyagi – without all the household chores of course.

Flow

This is some good stuff. I also enjoyed the weightlifting thread the other day. What you describe as a "streamlined consciousness" is something I've felt before many times during sports. I think mainstream calls it "flow" or being in "the zone". (I used to have some academic papers somewhere, but there's a ton of stuff on google – these guys are endorsed by Jimmy Johnson and Dan O'Brien).

Anyway, my experiences with this 'altered state' was reached very simply through self-hypnosis. Well, that's a little misleading because it's not exactly simple since the process involves the creative thrust of "giving birth" which is always more traumatic or shocking than "death".

So, for me to "give birth" to this altered state of consciousness what I did was similar to how I self-hypnotized myself to heal my myopic vision. When I wanted to fix my eyes, I just asked a simple question, "I wonder if I can get by without my glasses?" The question is the simple part – the birth of this idea into physical reality is what can be a little painful (high of amounts of blurriness at first when getting rid of the eye-wear).

When playing golf or any other athletic game, I just changed the question a little, but kept it very simple and asked "I wonder how many birdies I can make?". Again, the hard part being the attempt to birth this mental state into the physical world (because all the other "mental states" you've ever known are competing for your attention and you must learn to push those away and really, really focus on the simple mantra positive mantra of answering the question of: "How many of these can I get or do?"

And the more birdies, goals, whatever that pile up, or the closer you get to breaking a record – the harder it is to "hold" that simple focus because now not only are all the other mental states you've ever know competing for your attention, but now new mental states are crowding in – the mind looks at your current "score" and keeps creating new ideas and situations "Hey, look how awesome we're doing let's go tell someone!" (So, there's a little pain again if you really want to hold yourself in that one "space" or "state" of mind where you're answering the question you've asked and not jump to all the new questions that keep getting created based on how your game/performance is unfolding).

The moment of power is in the PRESENT. The thoughts you had yesterday don't matter. What you will be thinking tomorrow is unimportant as well. The only thing that matters are the thoughts you are having RIGHT NOW. And here's the thing. Don't freak out. It WILL look different than how you "expect".

Because if you truly have created a new thought-form or 'altered state' – it's new. You have no idea what it should be like – or have any familiarity with it. You might even scare yourself. But don't freak out. If you got the results you "expected" from the thoughts you had in the PAST – then that's just groundhog day and you haven't created anything new.

Connections Between Beliefs and Emotions

By Fire Snake| January 23rd, 2017|Categories: Beliefs, Emotions|Tags: Beliefs and Emotions

Here's where my logic is starting. This statement by Seth:

"The "negative" subjective and objective events that you meet are meant to make you examine the contents of your own conscious mind."

OK. So, I feel I've been relatively successful in unraveling one of my problems using this knowledge. It led me to uncover some deep beliefs I held that I wasn't aware of by following the emotions caused by said beliefs. (More Seth):

"Your emotions will always lead you into a realization of your beliefs if you do not impede them. Any emotion will change into another if you experience it honestly…fear is always behind hatred".

So, I was able to puzzle out that the hatred – and fear – I have of "limits" and "restrictions" was a result of fear from a belief in what the unknown/unrecognized parts of myself were capable of.

I think this is a 'good' fear though and a 'good' belief that I intend on keeping. I still believe restrictions and limits are bad after examining this feeling because people are always going to express themselves. It's better they do it naturally than be blocked and have nowhere to go with their expression other than through fanaticism.

Well, so after going through that mental exercise I wanted to practice again and at the time I was experiencing a bunch of feelings of confusion and bewilderment. So, once again I followed the emotion to see what belief was behind that feeling of astonishment.

If fear is behind hatred, what feeling is behind confusion? – disappointment, anticipation? (anticipation is the central ingredient of sex). Anticipation is also the process of imaginative speculation.

So, if anticipation is the process of imaginative speculation – and confusion is the result of thwarted anticipation – then what I'm encountering is "lack of imagination"? Then the belief behind all of this would be – there is never a lack or scarcity of resources or energy or imagination and that's clashing with the beliefs that things are scarce? There can only be so much money, or only a few smart people, etc., etc.

Scarcity vs Abundance mindset. Two people looking at a Rorschach ink blot and seeing completely different worlds. Half full-Half Empty. But it's *entirely* in the mind. These are beliefs projected outward onto people, places and things – and inkblots.

Anyways, I had such good results with these two practice exercises I went ahead and did it again and followed an emotion I was having of anger.

The emotion preceding anger in my case seemed to be disappointment. And disappointment is the failure of expectations to manifest. The belief I held behind the emotion of disappointment and then anger is that hard work should manifest itself in some way. Obviously, this was not happening. Just like the abundance/scarcity clash – somehow my belief that hard work should manifest was clashing with someone else's belief that hard work should not manifest.

Acceptance and Rejection

I was going to make a post about how to tell when you've been accepted by 'your people', whoever they may be, because I thought you could just tell by the way it "felt".

Like, pretty simple to tell when you've been "accepted" among your people – you feel it right? It's a feeling? Why people are scared of public speaking because they don't know if what they say will be "accepted", or if they will feel "rejected" by what happens. Also, why people are hesitant about dating and stuff, like will this person "reject" me? These are feelings. Feelings of rejection and acceptance.

So, that got me thinking. OK. What's the belief behind that feeling that makes you feel accepted? What do people "believe" will happen to make them FEEL accepted? And here's what I've come up with. Change. People "believe" something has to CHANGE in order to feel accepted. (And this goes back to my double negative stuff – and how we like to see the world in opposites) (And also the disordered nature of time but later…).

People need to "see" something CHANGE before they will accept it. Or before they will feel accepted. (I think I mentioned before I wasn't an emotional guy…) This is why people didn't take my magic seriously until I started effecting things in the "real world" they could SEE. If they could see the change then it made them FEEL accepted. Because they "believed" if they saw change they would have that FEELING OF ACCEPTANCE (and here's where time gets disordered…and math goes prime numbers only…and sex…and sigils…and aliens).

So, when my actual physical eyeballs changed shape and my vision healed. That made people FEEL accepted. There was a "change". Because of a belief in change. And when I kept pulling royal flushes when I gambled for a living. People could "see" that CHANGE. There were piles of money. It made people FEEL "accepted". And again when I demonstrated my golf skills and shaft bending prowess. You can literally see the CHANGE in the photographs. This made people FEEL "accepted".

Here's the thing (or one of the things). Which comes first though? The belief or the emotion? If you want change – which is the reason we're all here studying the occult right? We want to see some type of change? So, which do we focus our concentration on the belief or the emotion? The chicken or the egg? Can you believe without feeling? Without feeling a sense of acceptance? Do we need to believe in a change before there actually is a change? Oh my, what a can of worms.

People do this all the time though yeah? "Fake it" until you "make it"? Somehow these people have come to believe in "disordered time" where the FEELING OF ACCEPTANCE comes before seeing the CHANGE. I don't want to get crude – this is also how sex works – and hence sigils.

I'm sorry, but you're not going to "get off" without having a FEELING OF ACCEPTANCE first. People browse certain categories of porn. Why? They already know what they're looking for (disordered time – result before action). HOW DO THEY KNOW? How do they know something will "get them off" or make them FEEL ACCEPTED? Was it the belief or the emotion? Well, they knew before they browsed so…

That's why you can "believe" all you want. Use other people's beliefs in place of your own even. They won't do any good if you can't generate the emotion or the feeling of acceptance on your own – FIRST. Oh my god this sounds after school special. Anyways, this helped me tonight, maybe it will help you. Oh yeah – the prime numbers – that emotional feeling of acceptance you need to generate on your own – it has to be unique to you.

Also the aliens – Well, I wish I could take full credit for the above, but there was definitely some influence from somewhere because while I was out walking while thinking about this stuff I was like man, I wish something memorable would happen so I don't forget this and then a bunch of wildlife starting coming out of the bushes so…

Additional Resources

Austin Osman Spare and His Theory of Sigils,
Anticipation in Music

Symbols of The Future

By Fire Snake| January 23rd, 2017|Categories: Prophecy, Symbolism|Tags: Symbols of the Future

I can only speak for myself, but the struggle I'm working through right now is symbols/symbolism.

We were discussing "institutions" in one of the threads the other day and how they're not the best solution to ensure long term survival of knowledge and ideas. Well, if institutions are not the answer then what is? Why do good ideas fall by the wayside? My guess right now is for some reason we forget what's important.

OK. So, how do you keep people from forgetting? (I won't get into the why we forget here) but, reminders would help. Symbols are very convenient reminders. Especially if you can see them every day. Even better if you could use these symbols frequently or all the time.

If we look back at man's history, it appears to me there may be a pattern. Symbols always use shapes. Way back, they had pyramid shapes which we can still see and then more recently the big shape was a cross.

Here's what I'm thinking. These "shapes" or "symbols" are evolving – or – like we were talking about earlier they seem to reflect the focus of our consciousness.

What I see in those very old symbols is static shapes. Pyramids don't move. It seems over time our symbols or shapes have gained movement. Right now, we "animate" our symbols or shapes. We move these shapes with energy (gas, oil, etc) of various kinds depending on the symbol – cars, planes, boats, space ships.

What I also see in these older symbols or shapes is they seem to represent the "technology" of those eras. So, for it to be a good reminder, it should be visible and also usable (technology).

Let me try to tie this all together. Where I see symbols going next is the next step in the progression – static shape, moving shapes, and then after that self-animated moving shapes. How do you get something to move on its own?

You've got to impart consciousness into it somehow. (I'll do some speculation on how at the end, but this excerpt from Conversations with Nostradamus Vol 1 pg. 287 talks about some genius who is supposed to do this with 'artificial moons'):

"One of the things he envisions to help alleviate the miseries of mankind on earth is self-contained, self-supporting space stations. They will be like space colonies and will be large enough to be seen from the Earth as small moons.

As a corollary to this development, another thing he envisions is a way of transplanting some of his genius and knowledge into a type of organic computer so it will still be there to serve mankind after his body has aged and died."

This is some pretty good symbolism I think. An object in the sky you can see every day as a "reminder", but also usable technology because it's got some kind of organic consciousness computer "animating" it.

A circle or sphere or moon I think is also a nice symbol because it represents things like wholeness, all-encompassing, no sharp boundaries, inclusionary ideas and how consciousness is in everything.

OK. So, how is this going to happen? Right now I would describe it as a "technology phase change" that's going to have to happen. So, if you want water to boil, you need to add more and more heat.

Well, if you want technology to boil, you need to add more and more mental energy. This is happening pretty much without any conscious efforts on our parts.

This is what we seem to be doing without much thought. We keep directing more and more mental energy at our technology. So, if we have "static" solid symbols right now that we can only animate by adding fuel, gas, oil – the future should bring what I'll call "liquid technology" that moves on its own (solid-liquid-gas) once the mental energy threshold is reached.

Oops, I meant to tie all this back to the original question and say the struggle never ends. I think we all have our personal symbols and those change over time and our relationship to them.

Phase Change of the Spirit

I made a post a little while back talking about a "technology phase change". Which could be interpreted in a way as "alchemy". I also went through a near death experience that could be explained in alchemical symbolism.

In my latest podcast I talked about how the King Arthur story about the Sword in the Stone could be one way to look at my NDE. Another way to look at it could be like this:

My spirit or soul could be seen as the "water" phase.

And when the mental energy was turned up high enough – what happened was my soul started boiling and evaporated into the "vapor" phase of the spirit. Which then "condensed" back into the liquid phase when it found another body.

This is similar to how water evaporates into the clouds and then comes back down as rain. And this is why you can't "see" spirits or ghosts normally like you can't see evaporated water. The water is also in "two places at once" – it's location where it originally evaporated from and then it's location where it gets deposited as rain – bilocation.

Where did I get the extra "mental energy" needed for the escape velocity and to make my soul boil? Transmutation of negative energy directed at me. I don't care what kind of energy you throw at me as long as it's energy. I'll use it. Like the Delorean in Back to the Future II.

So, you can look at it as "alchemy" or science or even "yellow magic" as described in the Tao Te Ching – The softest substance hunteth down the hardest – turn yourself into water and you can carve canyons.

This may also be one of the reasons "heaven" is described as being in the "clouds" where water condenses from vapor and reappears as a solid.

And also one of the reasons the old prophets describe Jesus coming back "from the clouds". It could also have a double meaning and also be talking about "clouds" because they didn't have the word "internet" back then – kind of like how Nostradamus quatrains have multiple meanings condensed into them.

Additional Resources:

Saints who Bilocated, the I Ching Online, Conversations with Nostradamus Vol 1, Manly P. Hall on the Sword in the Stone

Science Is the Activity of Looking for Truth

By Fire Snake| January 27th, 2017|Categories: Beliefs, Science|Tags: Science and Truth

I figured I'd make a post about Science since it seems there's a lot of confusion about it and similar things like alternative "facts" or "news".

And while I feel I'm qualified to comment having "officially" studied Science at a high level for over a decade, I don't see this as a necessity.

Science is an "activity". If you look up the definition in the dictionary it says science is a noun – which is a person, place or thing. It's definitely not a person or place. So, we're left with science being a "thing". And the specific "thing" the definition describes is an *activity*:

"The intellectual and practical *activity* encompassing the systematic study of the structure and behavior of the physical and natural world through observation and experiment."

So, science is an activity just like any other activity like a football game. And I think a football game is a good comparison because at the end of a football game you have "data" or the "score". Just like at the end of Scientific activity you will also have "data".

This is where I think people start to get confused though. The "data" or "facts" or "score" of the activity or football game are not Science. They can be regarded as Scientific "facts", since they were the result of the activity of Science, but these "facts" or "data" are not Science itself.

Similar to how every single person will interpret the "score" of a football game differently (the refs screwed up, if only we didn't have so many injuries, etc, etc). The Scientific "facts" will also be interpreted differently by every single person.

The reason they will be interpreted differently goes back to a post I made the other day about "beliefs". Every single person has different "beliefs". And these "beliefs" are the lens through which the football score or the Scientific "facts" will be interpreted.

There are no "Answers" or "Science" just sitting out there waiting to be revealed. The only thing the Scientific method can do is "look" at things. And in my opinion, continuing to "look" at the material world through a pretend "objective" viewpoint has run its course and it' time for something different.

If we continue to look for smaller and smaller particles that make up nature. Guess what? We *will* find smaller and smaller particles because that's what we went *looking for*.

If we continue to look farther and farther out into the Universe to see what's there. Guess what? We *will* find a never ending amount of things farther and farther out there.

So, we've *looked* or examined the so-called "objective", or material world exhaustively. We've looked far. We've looked sub-atomically small. And we've found exactly what we we're looking for based on our beliefs about "how the world is".

I am not saying, "Let's get rid of Science". What I am saying is, "I think our gaze is focused on the wrong things." The truth is, at the end of the day – the world is a subjective place. When *this* fact is finally recognized, I think there will be less arguing about Science. You would not try to "force" your beliefs onto anyone else. So, why would you try to "force" your "interpretation" of Science on anyone else?

To wrap it up. The world is subjective. So, if we want to study "the world", wouldn't it make sense to study "the subjective" or look inward to the source?

Science is the activity of looking for the truth. We don't need a government, or a lab, or any person to "tell us" how we should be looking for the truth. This is the equivalent of trying to force a "viewpoint" or "belief" on another person. It will never work.

Keep Looking Friends.

Additional Resources

Dennis Overbye's essay about Science in the NY Times. Jane Roberts – The greatest scientific discoveries are always "accidents". Kevin Dunbar and colleagues estimate between 30% and 50% of all scientific discoveries are accidental

Who Is the Great Genius?

By Fire Snake| January 30th, 2017|Categories: Prophecy, Psychology|Tags: The Great Genius

This was a discussion that took place on the forums of the Above Top Secret (ATS) website. The topic of the thread was a Great Genius character who Nostradamus predicts in his quatrains.

There is an entire chapter (chapter 24 – The Great Genius) in Dolores Cannon's work Conversations with Nostradamus describing this person. The series is a trilogy with 3 volumes and they are awesome books.

I plan on doing some articles in the future on some other topics in those Nostradamus books, but the conversation that took place on ATS was specifically about this Great Genius person. Regardless if it's true or not, it's fascinating to think about.

One of the stranger things about the whole project. The author, Dolores Cannon, said that after she started getting this material and talking about it with other people, a lot of them said they were getting similar material. Jeane Dixon was one if I remember right, and she has her own book My Life and Prophecies (I haven't read it myself yet).

I have read Conversations with Nostradamus a couple times now. I originally read them a few years ago and then went back to them when I was on a camping trip out West. Anyways, here's what I contributed to that discussion:

I read these books a little while ago and after getting over the indigestion from the future that was portrayed I'm going back through them a second time and figured I'd give my thoughts. I realize this is an older thread and there's also another thread here.

Anyways, here's my armchair psychological profiling:

My opinion is the most important trait to possibly tracking this guy down is given in the translation of quatrain Century IV-31 (Vol 1 pg. 286) where Nostradamus describes him as:

"He says this gentle man made the decision to use his genius to help rather than to hurt mankind, so he is always inventing and envisioning things that will help man."

They keyword here is – gentle. I believe this is the reason they say he will not be widely known until after all the destruction. Surely, this guy could rise to the top of any organization with the genius he's supposed to have. In an economy and culture and society based on war – there is literally no place for him, no jobs to be had that would align with his beliefs or principles of the world being a good place.

The second part of that description is also highly important to figuring out this guy's character, "to help rather than to hurt mankind". Man, what kind of restraint does it take to have the kind of power this guy has and use it to help people? What's that saying about absolute power corrupting? Way easier to confuse and fool people than to help in my opinion.

The next most important clue would then be found in Century IV-14 (Vol 2 pg. 233) where Nostradamus explains:

"There will be a leader born after the time of troubles who will be young for his age, but an advanced being. He is the embodiment of a great spirit."

Now, this is a remarkably strange phrase – young for his age. But also an advanced being and a great spirit? How is this possible? How is someone young for their age? Obviously people will say it just means "immature". Yes, I would agree in part. But Nostradamus symbolism always goes way deeper than that. That's why his work has survived so long. He says himself that almost all his quatrains are talking about multiple events because history moves in spirals – so they apply to past, current *and* future events. But also there's multiple events *within* each symbol.

So, 'immature' is one of the symbols, but if you follow it deeper I think it also relates to the reasons he won't be widely known early in his life. What do most people who finally escape from a cult say? They say stuff like, "I feel like I'm starting a new life, or I'm starting all over again with nothing". Someone getting out of a cult at around age 35, would indeed fit the description of a person who was "young for their age" (but also an advanced being).

I'm not trying to make this guy sound like a victim. I believe he chose those circumstances to incarnate into for several reasons. If you were a great spirit or advanced being who came here to make significant changes to the world through your work – what better place to study than a fairly popular cult who also have big ideas about significantly changing the world. This would give him a front row seat to see the ways in which big radical ideas failed to gain mainstream traction.

This is also probably where he will get a lot of the knowledge in order to unify physics and metaphysics. He's going to need first hand occult experience. The cult also answers the dilemma of why he's unknown early in life. Do you know how hard it would be to suppress the level of genius this guy is alleged to have so he wouldn't be known? You're talking suppression on the level of entire communities and cities of people. Suppression on that scale can only take place in a somewhat popular cult.

Of course, if he wanted with his genius he could overthrow and rise to the top if he desired – but now we're back to clue #1 – gentleness. I'm sure he realizes the means must reflect the end and you cannot have a goal of peace and use war to achieve it.

Lastly, I'd look for this guy around the Seattle area. This Quatrain was from Vol 3 (I don't know the page number my Kindle just says 'location 7368 out of 9042' so that's 80% of the way into the book):

"A new ruler anointed, rises from the 50th latitude; renews the once great fish. Peace for a millennium."

Seattle is 49th latitude North – so close enough to 50 and who knows with the earth shift. But if this genius is going to be involved with Computers and Biotech that's one of the places you'd want to be – Seattle.

America is also home to several very popular cults. Also Nostradamus says the Space Program will relocate to the Pacific North West during or after the 'troubles'. So, I'd imagine if this Genius guy is launching organic computer driven satellites into space he'd want to be near the Space Program.

There are several other cities that lie on the 50th Parallel North, there's a few big ones in Europe, but it's pretty certain in my mind this guy will have to come from America to have the kind of freedom to create that Nostradamus is talking about because it sounds like Europe is going to be a battleground.
Additional Resources

There's quite a few websites you can read excerpts from Conversations with Nostradamus if you want to know more here is a good one and here is another good site. This website has a database of all the Quatrains without interpretations.

I wanted to add a few sentences here that I had written a while ago that apply to the Aristotle quote about "madness":

There is actually a fear of knowledge. This is why there is the saying "all genius is touched with madness". What people are really saying is they're scared of the mind and knowledge is somehow dangerous. Basically, if you choose to pursue knowledge you will go mad because knowledge is scary.

It's not just knowledge that our society has tried to tell us is scary and dangerous. They also say emotions are scary and dangerous and can't be trusted. And sexuality is scary and dangerous. In fact, humans themselves are by nature scary and dangerous and you need to focus on "surviving" at all costs because everyone and everything is out to get you.

A Nostradamus Conspiracy Theory

By Fire Snake| January 30th, 2017|Categories: Prophecy, Translations|Tags: US Russia War

In my last post about the Great Genius I talked about wanting to cover some of the other topics that were brought up in the Conversations with Nostradamus material.

I noticed some things before the election last year that I pointed out in a thread on Reddit. Quatrain Century V-75 talks about a billionaire who, "will rise high over his wealth", and I had suspicions it could be Ted Turner or even Donald Trump – which is the direction a lot of the comments took.

It was interesting to discuss at the time, I thought at least. So, another 'coincidence' or 'synchronicity' I noticed going through the Nostradamus material was not just about elected leaders, but also relations between the US and Russia. And it's interesting this is happening right behind the "surprising" Trump victory.

The picture that some groups are trying to paint is Trump is somehow a puppet or under the influence of Russia. Well, the question that should be asked then I think is, "If Russia is influencing Trump, who is influencing Russia?"

And I think this is where our friendly neighborhood prophet Nostradamus can help shed some light. He not only says outright, in black and white, that the US and Russia will be at war. But he also gives hints as to how exactly this will unfold.

Here is the "war" proclamation from quatrain Century IV-95:

The realm left to two they will hold it very briefly,
Three years and seven months passed by they will make war:
The two Vestals will rebel in opposition,
Victor the younger in the land of Brittany.

D: The translators say that the two powers will be America and Russia and they will go to war at some time in the future.

B: America and Russia will be at war in the future, but this particular quatrain does not refer to that.

And here is where he talks about how this war will happen through guile and trickery in quatrain Century III-95 (This is from Chapter 14 – The Coming of the Anti-Christ in Conversations with Nostradamus):

The law of More will be seen to decline:
After another much more seductive:
Dnieper first will come to give way:
Through gifts and tongue another more attractive.

B: This has to do once again with the beginning of the career of the Anti-Christ "The Moorish law will be seen to fail," indicates that the Anti-Christ, in addition to shaking up the Christian religion and helping to destroy it, will also be shaking up the Islamic religion. The way of living and of conquesting that this Anti-Christ has will be a replacement for religion, and this will assist him in his conquest. The Dnieper represents Russia because it is a river in Russia.

Russia will be his first major Asian conquest and he will not do it through force but through guile, through the limberness of his tongue. He will trick the Russians so they will come under his power and there will be nothing they can do about it.

Since he comes from the Middle East, that area will already be fairly under his power before he tackles Russia. Then he'll turn to China and bring China and the rest of the Asian continent under his control. At that time, he knows he will be in a position to take over the rest of the world.

Basically, this guy's whole plan revolves around destabilization so he can take over more easily. So, if you look at his goal = destabilization. He *already* has the Middle East under his control, or right where he wants them.

And if destabilization his is immediate goal before military action, then he's going to want to destabilize not just the Middle East, but everyone else – Russia, China and the United States.

So, if you follow the chain of influence – what people are seeing with our newly elected President – they're reporting "surprise". And people are then pointing the finger at Russia – claiming they're responsible for our "surprise" President. Well, take it a step further then. Who is responsible for the "surprise" Russian influence on our "surprise" President?

Could that 3rd "surprise" finger be pointing to an Anti-Christ that eventually plans to conquer both the US and Russia creating the "destabilization" he needs?

This is still Chapter 14 – The Coming of the Anti-Christ – Quatrain Century I-50:

From the three water signs will be born a man
who will celebrate Thursday as his holiday.
His renown, praise, rule and power will grow
on land and sea, bringing trouble to the East.

B: He will be a threat to all, but particularly to the East because he will be successful in conquering both China and Russia, and will have the entire Asian continent under his control. He says this will be the first and only time that the entire continent has ever been under one leader.

Another excerpt from Chapter 14 Quatrain Century X-75:

Long awaited he will never return
In Europe, he will appear in Asia:
One of the league issued from the great Hermes,
And he will grow over all the Kings of the East.

B: He says that philosophy developed most strongly in Russia and China. The Anti-Christ, though from the Middle East, will take advantage of the aspects of this philosophy that allows complete control of a population. He will take advantage of that and develop a thought system of his own based on communism. But he will be able to work it in such a way that he will rise in power and take over to unite the entire Asian continent before setting out to try to take over the rest of the world.

Finally, related to this big picture speculation is the whole refugee crisis. Many people have reported this situation would be very easy to take advantage of by someone with bad intentions. Could Nostradamus have been referencing this in Century VII-7 (I've had a lot of synchronicities with the number 7 recently and I may talk about it in my camping trip):

Upon the struggle of the great, light horses,
it will be claimed that the great crescent is destroyed.
To kill by night, in the mountains, dressed in
shepherd's' clothing, red gulfs in the deep ditch.

B: He says this refers to stealthy attacks. The Anti-Christ's forces in the Middle East will disguise themselves as countrymen of the country they are trying to take over or destroy. The way they will be dressed and the way the will appear, the other countries will underestimate them and think them harmless.

Additional Resources

More Quatrains talking about the conflict between the US and Russia: Century II-35, Century II-89. Quatrain discussing how the Russians sent a manned space mission to Venus: Century IV-28. A fascinating take on the Cuban Missile Crisis and how close we came to war: Century V-78.

Introduction to Astral Projection

By Fire Snake| February 13th, 2017|Categories:
Consciousness, Meditation|Tags: Astral Projection

There's a lot of practical instruction hidden in Carlos
Castaneda's work. Maybe hidden is not the best word.
Because a lot of people are upset his writings even
exist.

This might be too close to a conspiracy theory for
some, but if you go and look at the overall pattern of
reviews for his books on Amazon. There almost
appears to be a "brigading" of 1 star or 0 star down
votes.

I mean, not just a few people. It's like large groups of
people are angry.

My suspicion is – there's lots of people making money
off similar teachings who are not happy Castaneda
made available these "advanced teachings" in a $10
paperback. (Some groups are charging hundreds of
thousands of dollars for spiritual teachings like this –
some are shelling out nearly half a million dollars to
get to the highest levels of Scientology)

Or it could even be CIA intelligence groups like I brought up recently. Because these "critics" are not addressing the actual content of his books – just the issue of them being fiction/non-fiction. They just yell "fraud" like they did to Blavatsky and Geller.

Anyways. I followed the advice of one of the better reviewers who said Castaneda's first 4 books are excellent and then there's a noticeable drop off in quality. So, I've only gone through those first 4 texts. (Someone brought up the Sinbad podcast when he was on "You Made It Weird" and he too has some good practical advice – along with the usual mentions of Robert Bruce and Robert Monroe).

So, the 3rd book "Journey to Ixtlan" addresses Lucid Dreaming and gets into Castaneda's famous "look at your hands technique". And there's a lot of similarities between lucid dreaming, astral projection and near death experiences – which I think I'm going to detail in a separate discussion somewhere.

But, the 4th book "Tales of Power" is the one that gets into Astral Projection. He uses the term "double" instead of astral projection though and here's some snippets of dialogue:

"Each one of us is different, and thus the details of our struggles are different," don Juan said. "The steps that we follow to arrive at the double are the same, though. Especially the beginning steps, which are muddled and uncertain."

"As you know, Carlitos," don Genaro said with the air of an orator warming up, "the double begins in dreaming." He gave me a long look and smiled. His eyes swept from my face to my notebook and pencil. "The double is a dream," he said, scratched his arms and then stood up.

A few pages later, a clue is dropped about how to specifically separate the "double":

"I was suddenly aroused by a loud noise and awakened. The noise seemed to be the sound of a shovel digging in gravel. I sat up to listen and then I stood up. The noise was very unsettling to me but I couldn't figure out why. I was pondering whether to go and check it out when I noticed that I was asleep on the floor.

"Was your benefactor aware of what you were doing?" "Certainly. He had been making the noise with the shovel to help me accomplish my task."

So, sudden unexpected loud noises while sleeping can create that needed rift or division or separation. People have also talked about planning ahead and having a friend call them at some random time during the night to try and startle themselves out of the body while asleep.

And if sudden loud noises can disrupt our normal "unified" consciousness. Then other sudden dramatic things besides sound can work as well.

From my reading, one of the ways Scientology likes to create this rift in sudden instantaneous ways is through hypnosis. One of the hypnotic suggestions Hubbard liked to give was to tell people to imagine their mind or consciousness at a point in space 3 feet behind their heads. And then once you've got your mind outside the body locally – you can direct the consciousness to other places farther away.

Another way to create a sudden instantaneous startle response without sound if people don't "believe" in hypnosis or astral projection. Go ahead and punch your friend really hard right square in the middle of the chest when he's not expecting it – like they depict in the recent Dr. Strange movie. Hard to be a "materialist" when you get the "wind" knocked out of you and can't put your spirit back in your body to even breathe.

Marvin Jones talks about getting the wind knocked out of him on this play and in this article. I've had the wind knocked out of me like that. You can't get off the ground not so much because you're in pain as you're waiting for your spirit to find its way back to the body.

What do you think they're trying to do in UFC when they try to make the other guy tap out? Those guys are trying to squeeze the spirit out of a person, they're not trying to do anything scientific like "cut off circulation and oxygen or blood flow".

They're trying to eject that person's consciousness. Knocked out. Sometimes kids play a game like that called "knock out" where they take turns intentionally make each other go unconscious by putting pressure on the carotid arteries. Some adults play a similar game to the children's "knock out" game, but adults call it "auto-erotic asphyxiation".

Same principle with anesthesia during surgery. Except instead of "knocking out" the spirit out of the body with force. You're displacing it with the use of various mixtures of gases instead. It's why you see a lot of people report spiritual experiences under sedation. I think L Ron Hubbard had an experience like that with Nitrous Oxide. Someone else I was reading about recently also had a Nitrous Oxide experience. Here's a long Rolling Stone article I haven't read yet myself.

Additional Resources

I wasn't recommending anyone punch anyone else in the chest. Actually, I would recommend against that. Because if you hit someone during the upstroke of the T-wave of the cardiac rhythm you can kill them. This is called commotio cordis.

And this is the Touch of Death referenced in Kung Fu as the Five Finger Death Punch or in Quentin Tarantino's movie Kill Bill as the Five Point Palm Exploding Heart Technique.

I'll probably get into this more later, but one of the reasons people like these "altered states" and their lives get changed by them is they have an "ecstatic" quality – especially NDE's.

And so, this is also why you get the French term "La petite mort" which translates to "the little death". An expression which means "the brief loss or weakening of consciousness" describing orgasms as "the little death" – because orgasms are also ecstatic like near death experiences.

The Seth Enigma: Archeological Expedition to Yale Library – Kickstarter

By Fire Snake| February 23rd, 2017|Categories: Archaeology, Consciousness|Tags: Seth Yale Library

About This Project

The Kickstarter link

For those not familiar with the Seth Material. Seth is a discarnate "energy personality essence" channeled by Jane Roberts and her husband Robert Butts for over 20 years from the early 1960's to the mid 1980's.

Their work together is enormously popular worldwide and has been translated into Chinese, Spanish, German, French, Dutch and Arabic. The material is regarded as one of the cornerstones of "New Age" philosophy, and the most influential channeled text of the post-World War II "New Age" movement.

Dozens of books have been published and the focus of study groups around the globe. What this project is interested in doing is examining the unpublished material residing at the Yale University Library where it is annually in the top 10 of most viewed collections. There are 498 boxes in the catalog there.

So, the request for funding of this project is strictly to cover transportation for myself to and from the Yale Library. What I hope to do with the material is several things.

Overall, I would like to make a documentary video of the entire event. And within the documentary, I would firstly like to give an introduction to the Seth Material for newcomers to his personality. This would equate to Act I of the traditional dramatic structure.

Act II I would then entail sharing of some of my analyses and conclusions of Seth's work to date (some of which are already available on my website as blog posts). And also reasons for my pilgrimage to New Haven.

The remainder of the documentary would then comprise whatever new material was found among the archives, and how it fits in with what we already know from his widely-published writings.

Obviously, I can't say for sure what the finished documentary video will contain. Only that there will be one. And it will cover his known work and also my journey to discover more.

Who knows? There could be an entire army of hidden gems just below the surface waiting to be discovered as Seth himself even says in "The Unknown Reality Vol 1" page 295:

"There are lands of the mind. That is, the mind has its own "civilizations," its own personal culture and geography, it's own history and inclinations…and true archaeological events are found not only by uncovering rocks and relics, but by bringing to light, so to speak, the memories that dwell within the psyche."

Here is the budget for the estimated breakdown of costs for this project. It will take me 3 days each way to drive from Florida to Connecticut (6 days of travel). And then I am scheduling 1 week at the Library itself to do the digging (I may be able to stay with a friend if it takes longer than anticipated).

So, 2 weeks there and back total. And the analysis and production of the documentary I hope to have within a month or so of return – May 2017.

$1050 Hotels
$400 Gas/Tolls
$150 Research Materials
$150 Production Costs
$150 Miscellaneous Travel Expenses
$190 Fees – Kickstarter/Payment Processing

Total $2090

Again, this is just the outline of what I hope to accomplish. There will be at least 1 documentary video as a result of this project. Possibly more depending on how it plays out. So, I hope you found some of this interesting and thank you for taking the time to consider my proposal.

Risks and Challenges

This is just a trip to the library (albeit one farther away than normal). So, there's not a whole lot that can go wrong outside of a major catastrophe.

Additional Resources

I have personally gone through most of Seth and Jane Roberts books 2-3 times each, so I feel I can offer a bigger picture view of the material than most people.

There's no source I can link you to, but I recall Oprah was big fan of the Seth Material as well, having read more than a dozen of his books back in the 80's. She was even quoted one of Seth's mantra's, "You create your own reality" back when "The Secret" by Rhonda Byrne was featured on her show.

For more information on channeling, Edgar Cayce is probably the most popular material outside of Seth. "The Sleeping Prophet" by Jess Stearn is a good introductory book and the Edgar Cayce Foundation is a terrific resource in Virginia with lots of information on their website – www.edgarcayce.org

Seth even comments on Edgar Cayce when he brings up the concept that knowledge does not exist outside of the person who knows it. Therefore there is no "Akashic Hall of Records" where material is stored for retrieval:

"Knowledge does not exist independently of the one who knows. Someone gave Cayce the material. It did not come out of thin air. It came from an excellent source, a pyramid gestalt personality, with definite characteristics, but the alien nature of the personality was too startling to Cayce and he could not perceive it."

The Streisand Effect and Schrodinger's Cat

By Fire Snake| February 27th, 2017|Categories: Consciousness, Psychology|Tags: The Streisand Effect

For some reason, I just assumed people were largely aware of this concept. However, a quick google search for the "Streisand Effect" only turned up 300,000 hits compared to over 800,000 hits for "Occam's Razor" (a defense often invoked by scientists). So, I felt the need to write a bit about it in a blog post.

I think the Streisand Effect also relates to something I was talking about in my Videocast #4 – Alien Intelligence Part 1, where I brought up the movie "Whiplash" and commented that greatness is something found within. I also mentioned this inherent greatness was something *unique* to each person and no "instructor" or "teacher" can tell you how to be yourself.

So, I had said I had some personal experience with looking inward because of similar situations in my life. The reason *why* I had to look inward to find explanations that made sense, I feel, is the "Streisand Effect" just dressed up in a different disguise.

Here's a basic description of the Streisand Effect from Wikipedia:

"The Streisand effect is the phenomenon whereby an attempt to hide, remove, or censor a piece of information has the unintended consequence of publicizing the information more widely, usually facilitated by the Internet."

For me, what was happening or what was attempting to be "suppressed" was my personality. I had trouble being myself because everyone around me wanted to "impose" or "force" their personality and likes and dislikes in place of my own.

And the more I was told there was something "wrong" with my ideas and thoughts and opinions that they needed to be silenced – the more I was forced to look inward to see what made these imaginings of mine so "bad".

This concept also calls back to another topic I've discussed in a few places, Scientology. One of the reasons behind the popularity of this religion was the "mystery" surrounding the upper level teachings.

The highest levels of instruction were "suppressed" or "hidden" from people intentionally in order to generate more interest – The Streisand Effect. And then we also saw this interest dissipate when these teachings were made widely available on the internet.

So, I want to look at the mechanics of the "Streisand Effect" a little bit and one of the easier ways to analyze this I think is through the Schrodinger's Cat thought experiment.

Yes, I realize the Schrodinger's Cat thought experiment is only an attempt to understand just *one* interpretation of quantum mechanics among the many, many interpretations available. (The Copenhagen Interpretation – you can read about other interpretations here).

Anyways, I'd like my article to be read by more than the 4 people in the world who are actually familiar with and understand all the interpretations so I'm going to have to stick to the fairly well known concept of Schrodinger's Cat.

And all these various interpretations call back to the mental law of the Rorschach inkblot test I've covered extensively elsewhere – people see what they want to see. (Blog Post: Connections Between Beliefs and Emotions).

It's no different than going to an art gallery and everyone taking something different away from what they see. It's just people like to dress things up and make themselves feel important with big fancy words or big fancy math equations.

Nothing wrong with that. We are all important. The problems start when people try to deny that feeling in others. More of the "restriction" I've described numerous times. Only this time a "restriction" in the range of emotions.

So, getting into it. What happens with Schrodinger's Cat is basically a scenario where a cat may be simultaneously both "alive" and "dead", a state known as quantum superposition.

And it's not until the box is opened to *look* does the cat become either alive or dead. It's both until it's observed.

Well, how does this relate to the Streisand Effect because you're starting to sound like a raving lunatic, Jason?

So, what happens in the Streisand Effect is the person trying to hide or suppress information has also *looked* at the information. The information is not "good" or "bad" in itself. Just like the cat is not "alive" or "dead" until observed.

But when a person *looks* at or *observes* the information it becomes something. And that something is whatever the person believes or desires it to be.

If they just left the information alone it's still everything or has to possibility to be everything. Once that observer determines the information to be "bad", well, people are going to be interested. Because – drama. (See Videocast #6 for more on the mechanics of drama and the importance of both emotional and intellectual understanding)

However, people would be just as interested if the person who looked determined the information to be "good" or "alive".

And this is in fact what is going on with the search for the "God particle" in physics. The search would be equally as compelling if the term used instead was the "Devil particle".

So, I hope this article is helpful to people. It at least helped me clarify my own thoughts while writing it, so there's that.

Additional Resources

The picture featured above "Scandal" is a song from the band Queen, and Brain May is also an astrophysicist in addition to a musician. For a terrific discussion of the dramatic structure in music – that I feel complements some of my recent videos and articles – see this Youtube video on the making of Bohemian Rhapsody.

Also, related to this train of thought are the anti-drug campaigns. For many people, myself included, the anti-drug education in school was a first introduction to the world of drugs.

I actually had no interest in "drugs" until these educators brought them to my attention. Then I became curious because of the drama. If they had just left the "information" alone – the drugs retain all possibilities – neither "good" or "bad" – "alive" or "dead".

As Terence McKenna who liked to quote Timothy Leary would say:

""There are no bad drugs. There are simply people who don't know how to use them. Intelligent people use drugs intelligently, and stupid people are going to abuse drugs the way they abuse everything else. And our function is to raise the level of intelligence."

Although I would amend this statement to use the word "ignorant" instead of "stupid" and "knowledge" in place of "intelligence". As I believe we are all extremely intelligent, but may not have been exposed to the knowledge we need.

So, rephrased in a short and sweet way by Mark Cox:

"Don't focus on the problem. Focus on the solution."

And the "solution", going back to the Streisand Effect and why people dig into "censored" things – is the free exchange of ideas and information.

For more on "solutions" see – Sherlock Holmes and the 7% solution.

The Way Towards Health – The Medicine of Laughter

By Fire Snake| March 1st, 2017|Categories: Consciousness, Emotions|Tags: Health, Laughter, Medicine

The Way Towards Health is a title of a Seth book. It was the last one published, but one of the interesting things about it is the writing and construction of it demonstrates several of Seth's teachings, especially non-linear time.

The book and its contents were actually conceived by Jane Roberts during the writing of one of her much earlier books, "The Unknown Reality" in the late 1970's. However, for whatever reason the book did not make it to market until finally being published in 1997.

One of the reasons I chose to use that title for a new blog post was because the idea of illness has been appearing in my life in various places, synchronicities if you will. And instead of concentrating on the disease or problem, I wanted to focus on the solution or Health instead.

And I'd like to try to do this in a fun and entertaining way.

So, I've decided to structure this article around one of the more popular comments I made on the internet recently in regards to a conspiracy involving Dave Chappelle and "shadowy" forces who worked together to derail his career (video presentation available here).

Here is the original discussion that took place on Reddit a few weeks ago, although the original conspiracy goes back to the early-mid 2000's when "The Chappelle Show" was at the peak of its popularity.

Again, I want to emphasize that this is a conspiracy theory. Hence, there is no solid evidence.

And what follows is pure imaginative speculation on my part as I have no connections to any of the players in this drama other than what I mentioned in an earlier videocast/podcast about suspicions with my parents and their involvement in Scientology and Operation Snow White.

So, the basic overall gist of the Chappelle Conspiracy is that a few rich and powerful members of the black community were upset with the way he was portraying their race and were determined to shut him down – at all costs.

And this last part – at all costs. This is how situations become "unhealthy". Because if you remember back to my 4th Videocast where I discussed the simple equation of Means = Ends, how you go about something *entirely* determines what the outcome or End will be.

In the case of "The Chappelle Show", one of the complaints the cast members had, among many complaints or "attacks" aimed at them – they were reporting:

"Illnesses were plaguing key members of the crew". (See website)

Now, what's funny about this is, I recently also had a "mysterious" illness. And so did a few of my friends who were complaining about feeling perfectly healthy and then all of sudden improbably coming down with "mysterious" flu like symptoms.

And so, if you read my original comment in the Reddit thread linked above, I brought up how the medical examiner in the Lisa McPherson case, Joan Wood, was yet another seemingly innocent person who started suffering unexplained illness:

"She told the St. Petersburg Times she suffered panic attacks and insomnia".

It almost appears Joan Wood was a victim of Scientology's "Fair Game" policy which states:

SP Order. Fair game. May be deprived of property or injured by any means by any Scientologist without any discipline of the Scientologist. May be tricked, sued or lied to or destroyed.

So, Joan Wood was for all practical purposes standing in the way of Scientology's very existence because losing this court case would have been the end of the church. And if you remember back to my Videocast #5, I talked about how L Ron Hubbard's son Ronald DeWolfe is quoted as saying:

"Black magic is the inner core of Scientology".

Well, if Ronald DeWolfe is to be believed, then all these "mysterious" illnesses make sense as a product of black magic.

Now, I can't personally tell you whether it's possible to makes someone sick with only your mind and thoughts because I've never tried it nor will I ever. But what I have done is use only my mind and thoughts to heal myself (see Videocast #2 – Miraculous Healing). So, logical extrapolation would say – if you can use these mental powers for Health – they can also be used for the opposite.

What I am not specifically saying is that Scientology was partly responsible for what happened to Dave Chappelle. However, the situation is clearly very similar in that it appears Chappelle was a "targeted individual" in the same way that Scientology declares or targets individuals with their "Fair Game" policy.

And since there are already coincidences between the two cases, Joan Wood and Dave Chappelle, it would make sense to look closer and see if there are any other.

As mentioned in my comment on Reddit, one of the coincidences on closer inspection is the link between Oprah and Tom Cruise. 2005 was the year of the couch jumping incident which was also right in the middle of the Chappelle dispute.

For me, it's just very hard to wrap my mind around the strangeness of a person like Oprah playing God or determining someone like Chappelle's artistic work was "bad", yet at the same time prominently featuring, promoting and publicizing the values of the Church of Scientology as "good" despite the laundry list of accusations against them (as an organized crime syndicate involved in human trafficking, government infiltration, white collar financial fraud/tax evasion, etc, etc,)

The only way the hypocrisy of situation like that would make any sense is if Oprah was also a Scientologist.

Which would not be that far-fetched as it is a very popular religion among celebrities of her stature.

They were even able to recruit Stanley Kubrick's daughter into the fold. With many people believing his movie "Eyes Wide Shut" was an expose of their workings and the reason he was killed or suffered a "mysterious" heart attack – with the final edit of the film taken out of his hands.

And then the last coincidence I wanted to point out before this article goes too far beyond my self-imposed 1000-word limit for blog posts, was the mention in the Chappelle story of his credit cards being shut down while trying to pay for lunch.

Scientology also has a sketchy history with credit cards in that American Express is called out in this thread on the ex-Scientologist's message board.

Among the points brought up in that discussion is that American Express was possibly infiltrated in the same capacity and manner they infiltrated the IRS and other government agencies as part of Operation Snow White.

The reasoning behind them wanting to infiltrate American Express would be to have agents in key positions in order to fraudulently approve any charges going to towards the very expensive Scientology course work, regardless if the applicant was a good risk.

I also have a strange personal coincidence with American Express in that my parents opened credit cards for both my sister and I when we were very young – around 1980 – that was explained away as, "Just a joke" – It's now been almost 40 years and I'm still trying to find the humor in identity theft and financial fraud? (This fraudulent opening of credit cards/identity theft was actually on ongoing "issue" throughout our childhoods).

Now, people will be quick to point out that when Chappelle was asked about the whole situation he explained it away as a "contract dispute". Which is not a lie, but I don't think it's the entire story either.

For those not familiar, when someone is "targeted" one of the very first strategies they use to try to make the victim appear "crazy" through various means. So, if you had someone like Chappelle even *introducing* the topic of black magic being practiced against him – he would be implementing their plan for them.

And I am also aware the original website the Chappelle Theory was featured on has now been taken down with the author proclaiming it as a hoax. But again, if there were a few powerful individuals who could silence a star of Chappelle's magnitude, then silencing and censoring a random webmaster would be a walk in the park.

Anyways, these are just some of my thoughts building upon what other people have already put together or pointed out in various other places. I may do a part II in the future if people find this entertaining or informative.

So, to reinforce a couple points and summarize. These are not "facts" I am claiming to present here. There are just what I find to be interesting "questions" or concerns about how we live our lives. And one of the questions I find fascinating taking all this into consideration is:

If laughter is indeed the best medicine, and laughter comes from within. When we complain about being "crucified" in our daily interactions – is it really something external crucifying us or is that also coming from within?

Additional Resources

Finally, I don't really have an opinion on "Pizzagate" because I haven't looked too far into it, but I did think the symbolism was interesting in the highly controversial episode "Oprah's Baby Daddy" (Season 2, Episode 9) of the "The Chappelle Show".

And so, I put together a little montage of what appeared to be significant gestures to my untrained eye as I have never been affiliated with any secret societies or the like.

(Please see website for images)

And actually, I have a policy against secrets in general that I adopted from Terence McKenna who said (at 2:18:27 into this lecture):

"I have a rule. Which is: I'm against any group which keeps secrets. And Gurdjieffians keep secrets. I'm not against Gurdjieffians per se. And in fact, it's kind of too bad they get into the category. But secret keeping is a bad habit. And if you tell me a secret I'll probably tell it. Nobody ever told me not to say anything."

I'm not sure *why* McKenna lived by this principle, but as I've said before my reason is because I want freedom of expression at the end so I need to be able to express myself freely as the means.

If you want to look more into Pizzagate on your own there is an excellent Joe Rogan Experience podcast featuring Alex Jones where they examine many of the factors surrounding that story

Written Transcript from Videocast #1 – Near Death Experience

Introduction music

OK. So, Fire Snake Prophecy. The questions you're asking are, "What is this all about? What am I doing here?" This is not about predictions of the future - earthquakes, assassinations, etc.

This is basically just a way, or a place, for me to share my thoughts, my ideas, my view on things. If you're happy with how things are and you like what you see, that's fine. If I can maybe help anyone, give them a different perspective, a different outlook on things, that's fine as well.

The name Fire Snake comes from the Chinese Zodiac. 1977, the year I was born. The year of the snake. The fire snake. There's other snakes - wood snakes, water snakes.

Which will end up being meaningless anyways, when we start starting about time and how it works simultaneously and you have past present and future happening at once. Similar to how when people talk about reincarnation and they talk about past lives.

There's no real past lives if future lives and present lives are happening at the same time. So, the concept of being born under just one astrological sign doesn't make any sense when you're born under all of them.

The same with the word prophecy. It doesn't make sense to talk about someone seeing into the future when there is no future - you're just seeing what it. So, this thing had to have a name. I had to pick one and Fire Snake Prophecy sounded pretty badass, so that's what I went with.

I don't want to talk about time right now. What I want to talk about is consciousness. Although time is a perception of consciousness. And actually everything ends up being a function of consciousness because consciousness is the primary building block of reality. And I want to start the discussion of consciousness with a near death experience that I had.

This material was originally intended to be a book. So, bear with me while I learn how to make and produce and edit videos. There is, if you're interested, a completed first chapter of the book available on my website at firesnakeprophecy.com As well as these videos in podcast format and written transcripts.

Before I get into the near death story, I do want to say a few things up front that overarch throughout all the material.

So, consciousness is the primary building block of reality. Basically, consciousness is all there is. And the end result of this is that your mind literally creates the world around you. So, your thoughts and what you think will be what you experience and what you see.

And it's kind of funny, I've run across quite a few people recently who complain about the untrustworthiness of other people. Well, if that's what you go looking for that is exactly what you will find. And the opposite is also true. If you go looking for peace, beauty, wisdom - they will appear. Your mind will make it so.

And I don't blame people for having trust issues. Our society, our culture, from a very early age, from birth even, give suggestions. Negative suggestions about the nature of other people, the ability to trust them, and their nature in general. And even negative suggestions about trusting our own selves.

And people internalize these suggestions and they start to think they need gadgets to do what their mind is already capable of. They think if they relied on their natural instincts, the natural grace they were born with it would lead to trouble or danger.

For example, you have people nowadays wanting to build a quantum computer. Well, you already have a quantum computer. Your consciousness is a quantum computer. It can operate at all places simultaneously and on all planes of reality.

Or you have people wanting to use a space shuttle to travel to different worlds. Again, this is just another gadget to do what your mind is already capable of. If you want to travel to different worlds and meet alien life forces just take DMT. Or any psychedelic. Actually, you don't even need drugs just go to sleep and dream at night or meditate.

And so people want to use gadget because they don't trust themselves. I'm not saying gadgets are bad or there's anything wrong with them. They're just things that existed in the mind before they existed in physical form. All technology exists in the mind before it's created in physical form. So, if you want a prediction of what future technology will look like, all you have to do is look into the mind.

Take UFOs for instance. They seem to travel through space and materialize from another plane of reality. Right now our space shuttle is traveling on the surface of space so it's highly unlikely we'll encounter any new worlds.

I want to talk about consciousness first of all and then later on get into time and space and suggestion.

So, let me tell you the story of my near death experience. Which was the most incredible thing that happened to me.

Which is saying a lot considering the miraculous healing of my eyesight, my lifelong myopic vision. Both of these things had one thing in common though. Which is all I had to do was ask a question and my mind went out and found the answer.

So, I just got done saying how your mind creates the world around you. You get what you concentrate on or you become what you worship.

Now, you're probably wondering since I had a near death experience, "Why was I focusing on death?" Well, I wasn't focused on death. I was focused on getting answers. And one of the answers I found is that death is an illusion.

Things cycle. They blink on and off. They don't constantly stay on. When you turn a light switch off you don't say the light bulb died. The same thing when you go to sleep at night. And this is how the whole universe operates. We just don't perceive it as such right now.

And so, the better question to ask would be, "Why was I trying to blink out of reality?" And I'm going to have to give you a little bit of personal history for this to make any sense. But the short answer is fulfillment.

Fulfillment is the reason we blink into existence. And fulfillment is the real purpose of life - not survival like some people would lead you to believe. And real fulfillment should benefit every other consciousness as much as it does you.

And so, throughout my life I kept having these repeating experiences where one heartbreaking thing would happen to me, but another opportunity would materialize seemingly out of nowhere and with almost no effort on my part.

This happened when I graduated med school, when I was playing poker, when I was writing screenplays and most recently again with golf.

And so, this goes back to fulfillment of yourself and others. I mean sure, I guess I could have just kept having these amazing, magical events or experiences happen to me and kept it to myself. But then what do I say at the end of my life? "Wow, what a bunch of awesome stuff happened to me?"

Wouldn't it be better if I could somehow figure out what was happening or how this works so other people could bring some cool, great stuff into their lives as well?

So, this stuff that kept happening to me. People call these kinds of things serendipity or synchronicity or whatever else. We have names for it, but we really have no idea how it works.

So, in my mind I thought: This information is coming to me from somewhere. There's a place where it exists before it ultimately reaches me. And it's not any place I can see in this world. So, it must be coming from another dimension or another plane of reality. And I need to go there.

And these are the thoughts that ended up triggering my near death experience. So, I needed to go to the place where the information was coming from. And as far as I knew, there were no instructions for how to do this.

I went through a lot of schooling. Nobody ever talked about traveling to different dimensions that I recall. String theory had crossed my path, but they make sure to emphasize its only theory. Well, I needed something practical. So, I turned to the only place I remember other dimensions being discussed which was the movies.

Now, I'm sure there's a lot of sci-fi books that deal with this topic, but I wasn't a very big reader until recently. There's actually a joke or story about the various doctor personality types. For instance, they call emergency room doctors the cowboys of medicine, anesthesiologists are the lazy bums, neurosurgeons are the egomaniacs.

Well, when I was in med school, I was focused on orthopedics. And the joke about them goes: How do you hide something from an orthopedist? You put it in a book.

So, that's a little preface or background for why I'm bringing up movies now. The first movie that popped into my head that I thought might help in getting to another dimensions was the movie 'Jumper' with Hayden Christenson who was also in 'Star Wars'.

In this movie he jumps to different times or places like Ancient Egypt, Rome or into bank vaults to rob them.

Short Movie Clip Plays

The more I thought about that movie though, he seemed to be taking off from a standstill from his bedroom or living room and it appeared that he was actually teleporting places instead of jumping.

I liked the idea of actually jumping somewhere though. So, another movie that came into my mind was 'The Matrix', specifically the jump program scene where Neo is trying to learn to jump from one skyscraper to another.

Short Movie Clip Plays

So, after remembering this scene from 'The Matrix', what I did was create a visualization in my mind of the jump program and instead of Neo I put myself there and tried to make the jump from one building to the next.

Well, in the movie, one of the supporting characters remarks that, "Nobody makes there first jump." And that ended up being the case with me as well. It wasn't a total failure though because something did happen.

I was able to generate a slight feeling of lifting out of my body, similar to how you might feel when riding a roller coaster. So, I thought - it's a good start. I just need to find a way to amplify that feeling in order to achieve total separation.

And for people who might think this is nuts. It's actually not. They've done laboratory studies of high level Olympic and professional athletes. They measure their body responses while the athlete goes through an intense visualization of their performance and routine. And they can produce measure physical responses as if they're actually competing for real.

And this is just another form of hypnosis or self-suggestion which we'll get into later. Many decorated athletes and world record holders have worked with the famous psychiatrist and hypnotist Milton Erickson. There are many books about him by both himself and others. And you can check my website for a list of recommendations.

But, back to the story.

So, I was able to generate a feeling of separation from this physical reality. I just needed to find a way to amplify or increase it.

I tried to run 'The Matrix' jump program a few more times, but couldn't get any further results.

And so I scanned my mind for any other movies which might help. And what came back was a movie called 'The Bridge'. Which is a documentary about the Golden Gate Bridge in San Francisco and people who go there to end their lives by jumping.

Short Movie Clip Plays

This last movie seemed to be a perfect match because I had lived in San Francisco for a while and could create a very realistic visualization of the bridge from my memories. And this turned out to be the key.

The problem with the 'The Matrix' jump program was that there was artificialness about it that was preventing full immersion.

And so with the Golden Gate Bridge I could conjure up all those small details that make a world seem life-like. The feel of the cold wind trying to knock you off balance, the sound of traffic and pedestrians, the space and distance to the water.

And so just like I had with 'The Matrix' jump program I went about creating a visualization. This time instead of on a building I put myself on the Golden Gate Bridge.

And I'm not going to lie. When I got up there I was a little scared. Because I started thinking about something else they said in 'The Matrix' which was that: "If you die in the Matrix, you die in real life".

And this is also the entire premise behind 'The Nightmare on Elm Street' franchise with Freddy Krueger.

Being up there on the bridge was so scary in fact, that the first time I jumped I had to abort out of the visualization because the feelings were just too intense. Just like how all the details of the environment had become life-like and real, the feelings of panic, regret and fear on the way down had become just as real.

The second attempt was just as nerve wracking as the first. Even though intellectually I had convinced myself that it didn't matter, there were still the feelings that go along with knowing it's going to happen.

After a certain point though there was an inevitability about it and nothing I could do would change the result. But, the last few feet before I hit the water came the biggest shock of my life.
There was a sudden burst of light, and what happened next I can only describe as getting ejected not only out of visualization, but out of my physical body as well.

So, in the blink of an eye I went from falling incredibly fast towards the water beneath the Golden Gate Bridge to floating leisurely above an unrecognizable new reality.

Before I get into any specific observations of this surreal new environment. I think it's important to take note of the speed aspect, both before and after the transition because it's going to play a part in how I try explain what happened. The reentry phase will be another important aspect to pay attention to.

So, at first what stood out most was the abruptness of the transition. It wasn't smooth or gradual at all. The only analogy I can come up with and it's not a very good one would be to go from watching a movie to getting attacked by a shark.

And the reason it's not a good analogy is because at least you know what a movie is and you know what a shark is. This was not a new situation or a new place, this seemed to be an entirely new type of existence.

The shark attack analogy also fails to capture the essence of it because it implies things like fear and violence.

Which highlights the second thing that stood out most: There was an overwhelming feeling of peace and well-being. There was no pain or suffering. Worry did not seem to exist. I was not worried about my body or how I would get back to it.

Those are only concerns when reflecting back from my current viewpoint. In that state, I got the impression I could have easily go on to do other things without looking back.

Those were my initial feelings. And my thoughts were similar to the feelings in that there was an expansion and freedom of thought.

The level of understanding and awareness seemed increased. That little voice in the back of your head that's always second guessing was no longer there. This was no thinking required to understand things, because somehow you already knew stuff.

Now, I want to try to give a description of what I saw. But this is going to be incredibly difficult for several reasons.

The first reason being, I don't believe I had a set of physical eyes in whatever state or place I went to.

The second reason being, I'm trying to give a linear account of something where a lot of these impressions were happening simultaneously. Some people who have had near death experiences describe this as having '360-degree vision'.

The last reason for difficulty lies in the fact, that I wasn't in this world for very long so I didn't have a chance to examine anything very thoroughly.

With that being said, this is what I saw and how it played out, keeping in mind that what I saw could easily have been images generated from a deeper aspect of consciousness. I firmly believe though, that what happened here was my consciousness, either a whole or part of it, having an experience while separated from my physical body.

So, I went from a headfirst position approaching the water at high velocity and following a transition involving a flash of light, I was suddenly oriented upright and floating over a surreal landscape.

So, the first thing I noticed is that I was moving in the forward direction the whole time at a little fast than casual pace. Neither the speed nor the direction of movement seemed to be under my conscious control.

There was no sound or not much of it. There could have been the sound of a light breeze or air going by, but no music or trumpets.

The view below me was that of a valley or canyon. It did not seem to have a solid 3 dimensional qualities to it. Like I could crash into and not hurt myself. It's also possible, I was the one who lacked the substance.

There appeared to be beings of a wispy material that were floating in the canyon. Their precise shape was hard to make out due to the distance. They were spread out and numbered maybe a couple dozen or so. I guessed that they were beings similar to me because I did not feel like I had a body.

My focus quickly went from what was below me to the direction I was traveling in. The sky was painted with brilliant colors. Not a sunset, but the colors you might find in one.

There was no water anywhere. However, I looked to see if I could spot the bridge I had jumped from. It was no longer there, but rather than confusion I remember feeling amusement or wonder or astonishment or even all those feelings at the same time.

After looking to see if I could spot the bridge, I turned my attention back in the forward direction and there were two wispy beings in the distance I was approaching. They were closer together than the ones in the valley, and my path seemed to be heading slightly above them.

I was positioned between them, but more towards the one on the right. As I got closer, their shapes became clearer and the best description I can provide is of: large, whitish, semi-transparent flying stingrays with pronounced wings. They also had a faint glowing or luminous quality to them.

After passing almost completely over the top of them I began getting pulled towards the flying being below me and to the right. I remember not being happy about this because I was having a good time just taking in my surroundings.

The pulling also didn't seem to be occurring in a straight line either. It was almost a feeling like circling a drain and being captured against my will.

And the next thing I knew, I was back in the physical world. But when I returned to the physical world it wasn't quite the same world that I had left because my body didn't feel the same anymore. Or more accurately, it felt like I was inhabiting 2 bodies instead of just my own.

I had my body with all its familiar rhythms, but superimposed on that were the rhythms of someone else's body. Especially pronounced was the breathing pattern of this other body.

And it was difficult to adjust to this other pattern because it felt like the breathing pattern from a body much larger than my own.

And then it dawned on me, that I knew who this other body belonged to. It was the breathing pattern of my 300 lb. father who was in the room next door.

As I slowly started to comprehend the situation, I realized some difficult decisions needed to be made. The scientist in me wanted to stick around in both bodies and run some experiments on this probably once in a lifetime opportunity. Another part of me knew that if the circumstances were reversed, I wouldn't appreciate someone running tests on me without my permission.

So, somewhat begrudgingly, I abandoned both bodies and settled back into my own.

And so, that's a fairly comprehensive account of my near death experience. Like I mentioned previously, there's a slightly extended version of it in the first chapter of my book that's on my website.

I think I want to end the first episode here though. And then the next time pick up in this same place and take you through how I started to make sense of all this.

So, if you've made it this far I want to say thanks for listening, or watching or reading or however this material made it to you.

Written Transcript from Videocast #2 - Miraculous Healing

Introduction music

Alright. Hey there folks. This is Episode 2. I'm titling it "Miraculous Healings". Because that's kind of how you can look at...one way to look what happened with my eyesight. It's not the only way.

Anyways. So, I want to tell that story today because when people hear that they want to know the details. What happened. So, I want to talk about that today.

That's not what I originally wanted to talk about. Actually, the topic has changed several times. You can see right now I'm playing a video game. Initially, yes I said...the first episode was my near death experience and then I had said I wanted to get into the explanation of that.

But there's a few more...I want to push the explanation back a little...and introduce a few more pieces with this episode and then the next episode - Aliens, I wanted to talk about Alien Intelligences - that's why I'm playing this Alien Isolation game.

Then I wanted to talk in the episode after that about Magic. And then talk about some of the...some more stuff...beyond the near death experience and the eyesight and the aliens. There's some stuff beyond that I think I'm going to put into the episode after that...which would be the fourth episode Magic.

But then that episode will start to tie together a lot of this stuff that hopefully I've introduced in these first three episodes. I mean it will start to get tied together all along, but I think more of it will come together in that episode.

If that's how it plays out though. Like I said, I thought this Episode, the 2nd Episode, was initially going to be just explaining the Near Death Experience. And then it changed to...I wanted to do a Kickstarter...I still want to do a Kickstarter. I put it up. It didn't get the funding. It can always be resubmitted.

So, the second episode changed to that. Then it changed to...anyways. Right now it's (chuckle) healing. And it might have seemed random how this came to be the 2nd Episode or the order of it, but the more I look into this stuff I don't think much of it is random at all. I don't want to say anything, but...

I don't know, sometimes forces just conspire and so this is what I'm talking about (more chuckling). This is Episode 2.

The difference between this episode and the 1st. The first one I had a little bit of production value because I was out camping every night for 100 days, 3 and ½ months. So, I had some nice scenery and surroundings. The weather didn't always cooperate, but it was fun.

I'm going to get back out there, but right now I'm in a house so I don't want to just stand in front a wall and talk so I'm going to play this game, Alien Isolation.

I think this order of episodes ends up being good because these are things people are interested in. People have some concerns. But they have some small concerns, but they also have big concerns.

One of the big ones would be, yeah, "What happens when I die?" So, that was kind of talked about in the 1st Episode, or the topic was introduced in the 1st Episode. I want to get more into it later on.

But that…so that's obviously a biggie, "What happens when I die?" And then I think another one of the big questions is, "While I'm here how can I enjoy myself the most? How can I stay healthy? And happy?" So, I think covering healing in this episode addresses that big question.

And then I'm thinking the next episode with aliens, another big question after, "What happens when I die? How do I enjoy myself while I'm here?" People want to know, "Are we alone in our existence?" Yeah like, "What's out there?"

So, I've had several experiences with…I'm using that in a real broad definition when I say alien intelligences. I'm just using the very generic term of alien just to mean different, but also intelligent.

That can mean a lot of things. That's why I think the story is important to flesh that out. But also stories are important for a lot of reasons. Symbols and symbolism are really…I guess powerful…that sort of covers it. But there's more to it than that.

Anyways. Healing. Miraculous Healings. Well, here's the thing…when I say…it might come across like I'm being arrogant or something. Like, "MIRACULOUS HEALINGS!" But part of my whole reason for doing this is truth. Looking for truth.

And if I tried to downplay some of these things that have happened to me. Like if I said, "Not a big deal. Nothing real interesting or special happened there." That would not be the truth.

So, the healing. You could consider that a miracle - my eyesight. That's one way to look at it. Like I think I said earlier. And then the whole near death experience. There's several ways to look at that as well.

I think one of the interesting ways is the story of King Arthur. King Arthur and the Sword in the Stone. Excalibur, right? This is the story? Arthur was mentored or tutored by Merlin I think is how the story goes. I haven't looked in a while. And Arthur is supposed to…

Well, anyways. That's the story. The interpretation of that story. Manly P. Hall wrote an excellent book called the "Secret Teachings of All Ages". And actually...this is one of the books that was on the bookshelf of Osama Bin Laden when they raided his compound with the helicopter mission.

The "Secret Teachings of All Ages", so this is a book that Osama Bin Laden was interested in. It's a good book. A lot of people are interested in it.

But anyways. What Manly P. Hall says in that book is that what that story represents, the symbolism, King Arthur and the Sword in the Stone. Basically, the Sword represents the Spirit or Soul, and the Stone is the Body.

So, when you pull the Sword out of the Stone it represents pulling the Spirit out of the Body, or pulling the Soul out of the Body. And if you can do that...then you've got Excalibur. That's the name of the sword.

And actually. Someone else wrote on this subject as well besides Manly P. Hall in "The Secret Teachings of All Ages". L Ron Hubbard the founder of Scientology. He wrote a book called Excalibur, and he considered it his magnum opus.

I don't think…I don't know if it got published. But he's referring to the same thing Manly P. Hall is. Removing the spirit from the body. I think Hubbard talked about it in some interviews or lectures. He described it as something like 'exteriorization with full perception'.

Anyways. So, that's what I'm saying. What happened with my NDE. That's one way to look at it. I somehow pulled my spirit out of my body. I pulled the sword out of the stone.

For me to downplay that and be like, "Not a big deal". That wouldn't be true. And I'm not over representing that. I don't fully understand it and that's one of my reasons for talking about this stuff is to help understand it better.

So, I'm just putting this stuff out there. This is stuff it's kind of hard to keep to yourself.
The eyesight though. Yeah. I want to get back to the near death experience and a lot of that stuff later. But I want to focus on the eyesight right now because I think that's another reason for putting that episode here at #2 is…like the first episode with the near death experience…

A lot of people they could say...they could be like...
"Well, that's all in your head." Right? "You dreamed
that. Or you hallucinated that. Or delusioned that.
Whatever. That wasn't real. There were no effects in
the physical world."

But here's the thing with my eyesight. No one can
deny that's an effect in the physical world. I mean...I
have doctor records going back 30 years. I don't
know...I have records from 3 or 4 different doctors'
offices.

So, this is not a hoax. No one can claim *this* didn't
happen. But, here's the thing – the cause behind both
the near death experience and the eyesight – it's all
part of the same thing. That's why I need to introduce
several of these things in the beginning here so that
the picture will look better down the road.

OK. Hey. This is...so this is still the story of my
eyesight. This is a different day though. It's still
episode 2. It's still the story of healing.

And there's something wrong with my voice today.
My throats all scratchy. But I'm going to keep trying
to talk and see how this turns out.

Anyways. Yeah. So, continuing from last time. I did…I started to tell a few stories. And I wanted to emphasize that's kind of…all they are. These are just my stories.

And I mentioned how people have questions or concerns. I talked about the big 3 concerns…or not the big 3…just big concerns. You know, "What happens when I die? How do I stay healthy? And are we alone?"

So, yeah, people are asking these questions and I'm not claiming to have any answers (chuckle). I have answers. I have answers for myself. Like place holder answers. The answers can get better.

But that's one of the things. Everyone's got questions. And everyone's got answers. You can't get an answer from someone else. Not a satisfying answer. If you want the answer to be satisfying it has to come from you. It has to be your answer.

And it's interesting because, you know, somebody could make a statement. Somebody could say something. But every single person is going to interpret it differently according to them and their personality.

And one of the good books that I always like to recommend that covers this topic, that idea, really well is a book called "The Structure of Scientific Revolutions". This is by Thomas Kuhn. Here let me see if I can pull it up on the internet.

(Typing and mumbling)

Yeah, this is it. This kind of talks about what I was just saying. Basically, you can't ever really prove anything. I mean you can just make arguments. That's what Science does.

So, we just pick…we just pick what explanation we like best among all the competing explanations. So, we kind of chose the "facts" that we use even like Scientific "facts".

And he talks about a lot of other interesting ideas. About how Science doesn't move in a very orderly, gradual progression. There's like upheavals and new paradigms. Paradigm shift is what he called it. Where there's like a dramatic change in how everyone looks at things.

Yeah, it's interesting. Because everybody always wants "proof". Like, "Prove what you're saying!" You can have evidence. But you're *never* going to have "proof". And that's all you can have is an argument. You can make an argument, present evidence, and see what people think.

So, yeah, you know, I brought up Scientology earlier talking Hubbard with Excalibur. He also had…he talked about that concept as well. I think he had an axiom or saying, "If it's true for you, it's true." Kind of like how everyone has their own personal truth.

So, if you believe something to be true…I think that's kind of what he was talking about. That got a little off track from healing, but…the reason why it's important for me to point that out now is because I am going to be telling a lot of stories. I have a lot stories to tell.

I've also analyzed my experiences and my stories and I've drawn conclusions…but I do have a lot of stores. And so before getting into the details of how *I*…how *my* vision healed…this is not like a new thing.

It's actually pretty interesting. It's not a new thing among humans. And Hubbard's going to come up again here in a second, but among animals there's actually...snakes. Snakes can improve...here's the article I have it right here.

Snakes have poor eyesight, but can boost their vision if threatened. That's pretty interesting. So, that's almost (chuckle) shapeshifting. Shapeshifting reptiles (chuckling intensifies).

So, snakes can do it. Snakes have infamously poor eyesight, which is why they resort to sticking out their tongues all the time to get a sense of their surroundings. This is very interesting because this is going to come up again when I tell...the next episode, aliens.

So, it happens in animals. And in humans. What is this...? Oh, Hitler. Hitler had a bout of blindness. I think for a long time people thought mustard gas. I guess he got blinded for a while and his vision healed. But now I guess people are saying it wasn't the mustard gas.

They're saying it was a mental illness. They're calling it "hysterical blindness". Anyways, I guess we might not ever know the exact cause of his vision to go bad. Like we don't know why snakes have infamously poor eyesight.

But anyways…it healed…his eyesight healed. So, you got Hitler talking about that.

Then, like I said, L Ron Hubbard who he also had partial blindness when he was in the Navy. Yeah, partially blind. But I think he also…I'm pretty sure he claimed that it healed just like Hitler's eyesight.

I don't think I've ever heard how he did it. I just heard that he did it. He healed it. It would be nice to know the details.

And then of course you've got Paul. St. Paul. Paul the Apostle. His conversion experience. So, on the road to Damascus…I think it was on the road to Damascus…I think he went blind. And then they took him to…here it is…

"As he neared Damascus, suddenly a light from Heaven flashed around him. He fell to the ground and heard a voice say to him, "Saul. Saul, why do you persecute me?"

Yeah. So, for three days he was blind and did not eat or drink anything. So, then they took him to…Ananias…or however you say that…. Ananias went to the house and healed him. Healed his eyesight.

OK. Something like scales fell from Saul's eyes. That sounds kind of like what we were just talking about with scales and snakes. Is that a synchronicity or…?

So, yeah, this stuff happens. It's like history moving in spirals. But it's not just animals and people in history. This is going on recently. The Bates Method. People were using that to improve eyesight. And they were saying they thought glasses were harmful and never necessary.

And…who is this…Aldus Huxley supported this Bates Technique. And so this was the beginning of the 20th century…

And then I think currently there's…what is this 2012? There's a clinic in India. I think they might be using the Bates Method. "The School for Perfect Eyesight". And I think they claim they can do it in 1 week.

I don't know how they do it. Just like I don't know how Hubbard did it. Or how these guys are doing it either. What does it say? Relaxation? A lawn tennis ball? So, that sounds like their doing…exercises? Of some kind. I don't know.

Anyways. All I can do is tell you how *I* did it.

Well, and another important thing to know beforehand is that my vision…I think I mentioned…it was. There's different levels of myopia. So, you've got mild myopia less than 3 diopters, then moderate 3 to 6, and then high 6 to 9 and then extreme more than 9 diopters.

So, mine was mild myopia. That's important to keep in mind. So, what is was…20/200 in one eye and I think the other one was 20/150. They were both above 2 diopters. One of them might have been 2.5 and the other 2.0 or 2.25. They were both above 2 I know that.

I gotta. Hang on. I gotta do something with the cat. "Oh, hey." OK. So, alright… (cat hisses) …Stop! Jesus. (More cat hissing). Come on! (Cat now starts growling). Anyways, OK, so (more cat growling). Are you kidding me?! (More hissing and growling).

OK. I'm back. This place is a mad house. I think you heard that in the recording. That was my roommate's cat (laughing). The cat's not happy. I think you heard it growling. I'm going to…she's got 2 cats actually, my roommate. And they're both acting weird.

The one spends a lot of time in here…and that cat is sitting in the bathtub (chuckles). It's empty. But she's been doing that…both the cats are female. Yeah, I mean she's just been chilling in the empty bathtub.

I think I know why. And I think I know why the other cat is upset too. I think…well, my guess is I'm wondering if they're having problems with bugs or fleas or something. So, I just ran up to Walmart and I got some of the Frontline or Pet Armor.

I think my roommate was using something else. Something less concentrated. I don't think…I don't know…see I have a problem with those chemicals. I did something similar… (video game cut scene starts playing…I'm going to skip this. Oh, I can't skip this…I don't want to talk over it)

Usually, you can skip the cut scenes. Oh, shit?! What? (referring to the video game). Dude! Alright, well. So, if you looked at my website you looked at…if you looked at any of the gear I took with me camping.

One of the things I took was some of that concentrated Permethrin for like ticks and critters out in the woods where if there's like Lyme disease.

The problem is that stuff is toxic...toxic to cats. I think it's really bad for cats. So, I took it with me. You're supposed to soak your clothes in it and then it's good for 6 weeks I think. Like 6 times you can wash the clothes and I usually do laundry once a week.

But I didn't put it on the clothes. I wanted to see how it went. Wanted to see if I needed it. Because, yeah, it's toxic not only to cats, but those chemicals...I mean...unless those bugs and stuff are bothering me out there I don't see why I should just go annihilating them with strong chemicals if they're not bothering me. Right? Like, if they're leaving me alone I'll leave them alone.

But I had it on hand in case they were bothering me. But they didn't. So, I didn't use it. Why am I stuck in here? (Referring to the video game). (More chuckling). So, yeah, I don't know, I went and got it for the cats.

I think the one cat does have…she kind of has a bad reaction to it. One of the chemicals. She gets like nerve…I don't know what to do here (referring to the game) …she gets nerve…her nervous system gets all weird.

There it is (game reference). So, I bought it. I don't know. Maybe it's not…maybe she's angry for another reason. Maybe it's not fleas. But I was thinking the one cat's angry and the other one is hiding in the bathtub. I was thinking maybe the one cat is hiding in the bathtub because of the fleas too. I don't know. Nothing's bothering me. Nothing's biting me. I don't know man maybe they're just crazy cats (laughing) and I can go and return the…

Anyways. OK. So, getting back to the story. I was just about to get into my story because I had gone through a little historical perspective. So, for me what happened is my vision went bad around…it was 7th grade. So, however old I was 12, 13 something like that.

I remember it really well because I hid it for a long time. Well, not a long time because they do…the school I went was a standard public school. They do the screenings regularly. I guess every 6 months or every year.

I don't know how often they do the screenings, but I remember I was having trouble seeing the blackboard for a while. And I kind of relied on just looking at the people next to me and what they were doing.

And then when we had to do the screenings you had to stand in line, and where they tested the people I could actually hear what the people in front of me were saying when they asked them to read the eye chart.

So, when they say...like they got the big letter E... what is it Snellen chart? And so people say, "E...what's the next line...A, Z, whatever". So, I just listened to what the people were saying and just memorized it.

Anyways, after a while though somehow I ended up with glasses. I guess probably when...I think 7th grade that's around when you start getting into real detailed Chemistry and Math equations right? Like Algebra and Quantitative Chemistry and stuff like that?

So, that's about the time…and I'm wondering…one of the things I'm curious about is the whole timing of that. Whether the material and what I was being taught was part of what caused the…so, the eyesight is a symptom, right? Well, what's causing…what's the root cause of the problem?

And I'm wondering if it was because subconsciously/unconsciously I wasn't liking what I was seeing.

The education I was getting. And that was the expression of my protest or dissatisfaction. I don't know. I don't know how you would prove something like that. Or I don't know how you would test something like that. Right now at least. I haven't given it much thought.

There are a lot of experiments I'd like to run. The problem is experiments can get a little costly, and that's why I was looking at doing Kickstarters. I have a couple more Kickstarters I'm putting together.

Anyways. That got off track again. So, that's when my vision went bad. And it's interesting too that's about the same time my sister's vision went bad too. So, I'm wondering if it wasn't just stuff we were learning at school, but stuff we were learning at home that didn't make a lot of sense either. Like it was a combination of just an overall bad education – at home and school.

I don't know. I'm just speculating here. So, yeah, I got the glasses and I got the contacts. And I wore those all the time. Full-time from 7th grade until I graduated med school at...well, I wore them even after I graduated med school...I guess until...well, OK, when I first stopped wearing them was...yeah, I graduated med school at 26.

I didn't have any breaks in my education. You know, I went, high school-college-med school, that was 12 years' straight. So, what happened, and I think this is an important point, is that I was making a lot of changes.

Obviously, well, actually, what happened was...I graduated med school and I made a big change because I moved out to the West Coast.

I had gone to school in Miami for med school. So, I moved all the way across the country. I was looking for work, and I was having trouble finding decent work so I was working construction. And from construction that's how I got into...that's how I transitioned into playing poker.

I was playing mostly online, and some in person. And what that allowed me to do...so I was making a lot of changes. And here's how I think this works. I made the big change – I moved all the way across the country. I made the change, I was working different, very different, jobs than what I had been used to in medicine, with the construction and the poker.

The thing about using the computer and making a living with the poker was that I wasn't ever really *required*, it wasn't *necessary* that I be able to see far. See distance. I could very easily sit at the computer without my glasses, and then just put them on when I left the house to go to the store or driving or whatever.

And since I was making all these other changes...I think the way it works is...people have talked about this before with the Law of Attraction, things attract other things, so if you have good thoughts that will attract other good thoughts and good stuff.

And so, when you make changes it attracts other changes and the changes kind of start piling up. So, it's easier to make changes when you're already making changes. That's the point I'm trying to get across.

So, it kind of seemed a normal thing to do with all the other big changes I was making. So, the thought came into my head that, "I wonder if I can completely do without my glasses?"

And so, I just stopped wearing them at the computer. I just asked myself that question and just kind of let it happen naturally. (Chuckling) I've been walking around in circles here, I'm pretty sure (referring to the video game).

I just asked a very simple question, "I wonder if I can do without my glasses?" And I didn't make any plans. I didn't put any restrictions on how...on exactly how I wanted this outcome to come about. I didn't say...I didn't have any specific regimen of exercises I had to do 3 times a day or a special diet.

I just let it happen naturally. That's the problem a lot of times with a lot of things. When you put restrictions on things you can never find out what the real potential is of that thing if you set a limit to it. Because when you set the limit you're focusing on the limit instead of the possibilities or the potential.

So, when I asked myself the question, "I wonder if I can get by without my glasses?" It's a very positive...reinforcing...it's a very positive mindset...very open ended to possibilities. Not like, "I wonder if I follow these specific outline of activities?" I wasn't focused on activities. I was focused on the outcome.

And basically, what happened is at first...at first it was probably a little dangerous. Especially when driving. And I don't know if I would recommend driving or if you do make sure you know the area really well like I did.

My memory has always been really good. I think that's one of the reasons why school and academics came easily to me. Like I said, I memorized what the people were saying about the eye chart.

So, I lost my train of thought. I was talking about memory. Oh, about driving around town. I would be careful with something like that obviously.

And when you think about it…this is another example of self-hypnosis…or self-suggestion. Very, very similar to how I induced my near death experience.

And it's interesting. That's a word they use in the medical field, induced. Sometimes they'll do like…well, anyways…like induction. Hypnosis, when you're putting someone under they talk about hypnotic induction.

So, when I induced my NDE what I had basically done is self-hypnotized myself. And that gets interesting…what is that? (referring to the game) …that's interesting (still talking about the game).

Let me see what the time is running like on this episode because I think this might be longer than I anticipated already. Because I wanted to talk about golf. Because I used the same type of hypnotic self-hypnotic techniques playing golf.

You know everyone talks about getting in the zone or being in the zone or the flow state. And I also have…I used the same…I don't want to call it technique because there's not really any specific step people need to follow. It's more about how you look at the problem.

So, let me check the time and see where it's at.

OK. I think I have about 5 minutes left here because I wanted to try to keep this under an hour. I think what I have to say is interesting. But I don't know if it's that interesting where I'm just going to talk for hours and hours, at a time, about it.

I wanted to separate it into episodes, but within the episode I wanted to try to keep it as freeform as possible. Like the same way I went about with my eyes.

So, yeah, I need to finish that story too because I told you…I told you the beginning, the middle, but I didn't tell you the end of the story. Well, obviously you know the end – they healed. But, actually it came as a surprise to me.

I didn't actually know that my vision had gotten that good. I guess I must have known subconsciously that it had gotten better because things weren't as difficult as they had been.

The first time I got them tested was when I went to get my driver's license when I was living up in Chicago. After I left the West Coast, I moved across the country again to Chicago. Spent 7 years there (chuckling) and towards the end I had to get my license renewed.

And you have to do a vision test at the DMV. So, I went to...I took the test...I told them before I took the test that I wore glasses. But I didn't have them with me because I hadn't worn them in so long. I just put them aside and went about trying to answer the question, "Can I get by without my glasses?"

So, I didn't have them around with me. But I went ahead and took the test because you gotta wait like hours...just to get...in the waiting area there. And I didn't want to have to do it all over again. So, I went ahead and tried to take the test without my glasses and I passed it.

At first I thought, there's something wrong with their machine. There's some leeway there so the lines don't clog up. My visions probably not 20/20, but it's got to be better than it was at 20/200. So, I was like…uh…maybe it's a little of both. Maybe my eyes are better and maybe the machine…there's something wrong with it.

The next time I had it tested was to get my license again when I moved to Florida from Chicago when I was playing a lot of golf. And so, when I came down to Florida I had to get my license here.

This time I remembered what happened last time, and I didn't want to have any restrictions on my license where it says, "Needs to drive with glasses."

This time I didn't tell them I wore glasses, and then I tried to see if I could pass the test so it wouldn't say anything on my license about having to drive with restrictions. So, I didn't tell them and then I took the test and I passed it.

Well, the odds that both machines are off that kind of gets lowered a bit. So, I wasn't absolutely convinced yet either. I was like maybe…who knows…maybe both machines are messed up.

So, then I actually went to a doctor. The eye doctor. When I was looking to get...when I was playing golf I was looking to get some sunglasses. The ones I ended up getting, the Oakley G30, those are specially designed for golf. The G30 are like the pink lenses, and they're supposed to enhance the contrast when you're reading greens for putting when you're playing golf.

And I thought they did as advertised. I really like them a lot. I wear them for everything now. But I thought I was going to need the G30 in a prescription.

So, I went to the eye doctor at Costco I think. I think they have eye doctors there. Yeah, it was Costco. Yeah, because my mom was with me we went there together.

And the doctor was like, "There's nothing wrong with your eyes. They're 20/20." My mom was surprised. I kind of knew, but wasn't sure because I didn't trust the DMV machines. But they got those big machines at the ophthalmologist where they do the, "Is 1 or 2 better or worse?"

So, the odds that thing and the other two machines are wrong…And so that was about 4 years ago. Yeah, that's the end of the story. There's the beginning, middle, and end.

And I wanted to apologize again if the way I'm trying to structure these episodes to be spontaneous and freeform as much as possible without restrictions.

That bothers people sometimes. But, I do have a lot of my thoughts in structured, written format if you want to read…I talk about a lot of the same things here over on my blog and Reddit as firensakeprophecy.

So, I like how…*I* like how the episode has been structured because…that's how my eyes healed. When I took away…when I took away the restrictions of…if you want to look at my glasses as crutches.

So, that's what I'm hoping by taking away the…you know…that anything *has* to be done a certain way in this episode.

I hope that some…some strange unexpected things will…we might run into.

So, yeah…I think that…I said it relates to the golf, but I think I might put the golf stuff…and the poker stuff too…because there's a lot of mental tricks that go into playing poker.

I think I'm going to put the golf and the poker into the episode after the aliens. So, the 4th Episode I think I said I was going to talk about Magic. Because you can look at those things several ways.

You can look at it as Science because they have…I'll get into it in that episode, but the people at Princeton University have been studying random number generators that people can influence with their mind.

They've been studying that at Princeton for 30 years.

So, you can look at it as a Science. You can look at it as Magic…or you can look at it as…there's a lot of ways to look at it.

Anyways, I think that covers it. I think that's it. Alright.

END

Written Transcript from Videocast #3 - Camping Trip

Introduction music

Hey, folks. It might have been a while since you've seen my face. Since in the last episode, episode 2, I talked about my eyes healing, I was just playing a video game and commenting while I was doing that.

So, today…what I'm doing today…I'm going to try to make a couple new videos. One of the…well, here's the thing. I want to give an outline upfront (giggle) of what I'm trying to do. Or what I intend to talk about because…like in the last episode. I told you I like the structure of spontaneity and being unpredictable, and I feel like there's lots of…I feel that way of going about things…it allows…it allows unexpected things to happen when things aren't so tightly scripted.

There's a lot of things going on. So, today I'm going to be talking a lot, and I'm going to be trying to make several videos. I'm going to be doing a lot and talking a lot. And I'm not sure exactly which things are going to go in which video.

One of the videos I wanted to make was just to show people how I use some of my various camping gear because if you've seen on my website I have a lot of written reviews of the equipment and gear I've been using, and sometimes people like to see that stuff in action.

So, I'm going on a camping trip is what I'm doing. And what I'm hoping to accomplish...I'm getting ready to leave in a couple hours...hour or two here. I'm just heading up to Alafia River State Park not far from my house.

And so, as part of that camping trip one of the things I wanted to do is just some short videos showing me using my stuff. Unfortunately, one of the things I'm not going to be covering with the gear is my cooking...my stoves.

Because right now, I wish...I wish...I was hoping this episode would be a little more high energy than the last one. Same structure, unpredictable, but a little more high energy. I told you I had a scratchy throat when I was recording that last episode.

Well, again this last Sunday I started getting congestion and stuff.

So, that's probably...you're probably hearing some of that stuff in my voice. So, like I did last time I'm just going to try to work through it and see what happens and as long as it's fun and I'm having fun, that's one of the...that's one of the most important things for me. I'm not going to do anything that's not fun.

So, I'm expecting to have fun. Today. And Tomorrow. I've got two days reserved. Initially, I wanted...initially I was thinking I would probably need 3 or 4 days, but it's a very popular time for camping in Florida.

It's February 1st so you got really nice weather. Near 80's during the day, and then you got nice sleeping temps getting down into the 50's at night. The campgrounds are packed. I got 2 nights. So, I'm going to be heading up there. I got a check in time at 3:00 PM.

So, once I get done recording this little intro segment I'm going to pack up the car and head over. So, that's one of the things I wanted to do is I wanted to do a video of me using some of my stuff.

And also I wanted to get a little footage of the actual campsite. The Alafia River area. Do some sight-seeing and hiking. And hopefully that...that nice energy...that nature energy will help with whatever this negative energy that's been surrounding me.

Scary music plays over montage of various wildlife (5:13-6:17)

Epic music plays over footage from dash cam drive into campgrounds (6:18-6:37)

OK. Alright. I just arrived at Alafia State...Alafia River State Park. It's about 3:30 pm on February 1st and you can see I mentioned earlier, it's packed. These sites are actually packed pretty close together here. So, I don't know if I can be as weird as I normally am, but I'm going to try to...you can see more people over here.

I'm going to try to get some work done. So, this is my little spot. I'm at spot 18 here. And I'm going to go ahead and put the camera on a tripod, and you can see how I set everything up.

So, the first thing I put down is the ground tarp underneath the tent.

Epic music plays while I setup my equipment (7:42-8:37)

It's 4:30 pm now. It took me about 45 minutes to put up both tents. Setup my sleeping gear. The only thing I didn't setup I told you I wasn't going to bring was my stove because when I'm feeling lazy (or sick) I'll just pick up one of these pizzas from Costco. $10 bucks. So, that'll last a couple days.

Alright. Yeah. I'm going to take care of some small stuff and then it'll probably be dark. Start a fire. And then...

More epic music plays as I wander around Alafia River State Park (9:52-11:55)

It's about. Let me see what time it is. It's about 6:15 pm right now. I had some dinner. Went for a hike. About a 3-hour hike. It's a nice area. I took a bunch of pictures. I'm going to have to look through those later.

The deck is kind of stacked against me because there's a ton of mosquitoes. There's a little bit of road noise. All night pretty much. Yeah, I didn't sleep well at all and after that hike today I'm pretty tired. Yeah, and these spots are really…are real close together. At least in this part of the park. Walking around some of the other spots have a little more space.

So, yeah, you hear the car driving by. So, yeah, there's a couple of problems. I think I only got a couple of hours' worth of fire. There's always a little bit of noise. There could be a lot of noise with the neighbors so close.

Epic music once again over footage of a campfire (13:43-14:03)

OK. So, I'm back home now and that last short segment with the campfire. That's what…I never got around to talking about the alien intelligences. It's just there's too many things. Forces conspired. There were the mosquitoes. The noise and the spots were just real close, probably…

Yeah, so it just didn't happen. And so what I did is I just recorded the fire and I got about an hour footage of the campfire. I'm thinking maybe I'll just talk over that for the next episode…I don't know.

So, I got an hour of footage of the campfire. I guess I could play a video game again. You know, who knows? So, I do want to get that done in the next couple days here.

Other than that, everything I think...the whole...all the stuff I was interested in...I had my little outline about stuff I wanted to get done. Got to show my, some of my gear. Some of it, quite a bit of it, I just leave in the car. Like the water, my big 5-gallon water and tools and the food so it's harder for the critters to get at – just leave my big Rubbermaid in the car.

Who knows? I might do another episode on the gear. I don't know.

But, I got to see a lot of the park. A lot of the lakes and the trails and the...there's bike trails and horse trails and then trails for hiking. It's a real nice, a real nice area.

So, yeah, overall on the list of things to do, got a lot done. So, I gotta work on trying to figure out how to put together the alien story. That's going to be hard for a lot of reasons.

One of the reasons is because I really need to focus when I try to remember the story because it's actually surprisingly hard to remember than like an actual normal event I think. For a few reasons. One of them being there's not a lot to compare it to (laughs).

So, yeah, I'll get into that...I'll get into that in the next episode. But yeah, I'm happy with how it went and I hope you guys liked the video. Thanks for watching.

END

Written Transcript from Videocast #4 - Alien Intelligence Part 1

Introduction music

Hey there people. Welcome to Episode 4 – Alien Intelligences.

I guess you're only going to get to see my face every other episode because today I'm going to be talking over footage of a campfire I recorded from a camping trip earlier in the week.

If you listen to the last episode near the end, I was a little disappointed that I didn't get to talk about the aliens while I was sitting around the campfire because I thought it was going to be a good match with the material because aliens can get a little spooky sometimes, and sitting around a campfire telling spooky stories is always fun.

But it just didn't work out. There was just too many…too many things. There was a whole bunch of mosquitoes. There was a constant road noise from outside the campsite you could hear, and inside the campsites the spots were just packed real close together.

So, it just didn't happen. But I think actually this is going to work out better because if you look at the symbolism of it…what happens…what happened in my experiences at least with these intelligences or these alien intelligences is you get…there's almost like a…your reality…you almost get into a new reality.

You get detached or dissociated from the world that you've known. And so, I'm thinking that me commenting over a video from earlier in the week it kind of…it kind of matches with that symbolism of…I don't…I think altered state of consciousness might be a better word than detached or dissociated. I guess those are more scientific words. Words that science uses – detached and dissociated.

Altered states though…I do…there is some…well, OK. There's a ton of material I've got to cover here so I'm probably going to have to backtrack a bit, or come back to certain topics.

So, I'll get into altered states in a little bit, but as far as why I think this works out better. I think, like I said, I think the symbolism is better, but at the end of the last episode I was also commenting that for me, trying to remember the actual experiences – the details, the specifics – it was surprisingly hard.

Not like, not the general. You know if people see a UFO or something big and dramatic happens to them. People aren't going to forget that, but sometimes the details can get a little sketchy.

One of the reasons I propose for that is there's not really a whole lot to compare it to. Like, if you want to view it as an altered state of reality, there's certain altered states we're familiar with.

You know, having a glass of wine or runner's high or things like that. You've probably had hundreds or thousands of experiences with those altered states.

But some of the experiences I'm going to talk about today, there's really…there's nothing else to compare it to. You've just that one thing that happened, or the couple things that happened.

So, I think this works better for the symbolism. I think it works better for me personally to focus on telling the story and not have to worry about playing a game.

We'll see how it goes. I hope it's…I hope there's something to look at. I got an hour of the campfire recorded. I don't know how much I'm going to be able to get into alien stuff. There's a lot of it.

If you go on my blog I've written a few articles on aliens so far. I've got a part 1, part 2 and part 3 up on my blog. I don't…I'll see how I can fit that stuff in. I do want to talk about it eventually. This might end up being a multipart episode just like the blog posts.

So, you can check those out. If you're looking for some books in the book section of my website on UFOs…these are some of the books I've read about aliens. They're all good.

One of them that's not on here. There's a few books that I have to put up on my website. I've got to write the reviews for all of them too, but this one about aliens, "Missing Time". This is going to the into the story from my childhood because I did have missing time in that encounter.

But this is a good book. It gets a little spooky when he talks about the aliens and what they look like and the color of their skin and how it's kind of marshmellowy. The texture's marshmellowy with a greyish/white color.

When you hear strange stuff like that they call it "high strangeness". So, the stranger something is usually the truer it is.

I had a friend growing up who had an abduction experience, and he said that the aliens smelled like burnt Styrofoam. Which is interesting because Whitley Strieber, or Strieber (different pronunciation), I'm not sure how you say his last name. This story – Communion.

This was a bestseller I think in the mid 80's, but he also talks about what the aliens smelled like. And he describes them smelling like wet cardboard. So, you've got really strange reports – burnt Styrofoam, wet cardboard.

The Strieber story is actually where…that's where the whole pop culture phenomenon of anal probing came from. Saturday Night Live I think starting making fun of the anal probing thing. But that came from this story.

So, there's a lot of good books on aliens. This one is a three volume set. This is the middle volume. Really good. John Keel. So, these are all good. I haven't put this up yet, but this one is really good.

Altered states, yeah, I said I wanted to get back to this. This was a movie. "Altered States" was a 1980 movie. It was…it starred William Hurt, but it was based on the life and work of Dr. John Lily who did a lot of research into isolation tanks.

And so that's going to tie into…not my childhood story, but one of my more recent stories with shapeshifting. This gets into…this movie gets into shapeshifting. So, yeah, that's good.

This can also be about shapeshifting (referring to a web article about gardening and plants), and I'll come back to this, but here's another book I haven't put up on my website, "Rule by Secrecy".

This is another really good book. Actually, one of these reviewers makes a really good point…I need to find it hang on…well, what the reviewer points out is that…I can't find it. Anyways, he compares this book to Helena Blavatsky from the Theosophical Society.

She wrote a bunch of books. "The Secret Doctrine", "Isis Unveiled". "Isis Unveiled" was actually one of Albert Einstein's favorite books. And it's interesting that how he came up with his Theory of Relativity.

That was through a thought experiment. It wasn't through like actual physical experimentation. It was a thought experiment. Which, if you…if you kind of step back and think about it that sounds like mystical practice. Thought experiments.

So, you gotta wonder if…where is the line between science and magic if one of the greatest scientists in our history is getting inspiration from Spiritualist philosophy?

Anyways, OK, so, yeah. I just wanted to point those out.

Well, one of the things. I guess we've kind of been talking about the mind all along. With the near death experience and the…but, it's going to get a lot into the mind with this episode.
And I've written about this point a lot. I don't know if I've brought it up in the podcast or the videocast, yet.

But, there's certain laws of the mind...of consciousness. Like, people talk about scientific laws like gravity. If you throw something up it'll come back down.

Well, there's also certain laws of the mind. And one of the most important and simplest: you're going to get what you concentrate on. Whatever you're thinking about that will become your reality.

And the specifics of how that law works is. So, if there's an equation, right? You have something at the end of the equation that you want, right? The end. And people want to justify the end by whatever means necessary.

So, the means are how you get to the end. So, you have the means – you do something – and then you get your result at the end. Well, people incorrectly believe that they can do "whatever" as far as the means to accomplish the goal.

So, if their end or their goal is peace, a lot of people mistakenly believe they can use war to achieve peace. Which is...you can't...it won't happen. It's like trying to violate a law of physics. If you want peace at the end the means has to be peaceful. It's just how the world works.

So, this has to do with the mind. These are laws of the mind. So, it's...yeah (chuckling)...if you ever have a boss or manager who says like, "Just do whatever it takes, I just want it done".

That person who says that - they don't know what they want, or they don't care what they get at the end. Or else they wouldn't say, "You would do whatever it takes if you really wanted it".

No. That's not true. That person doesn't know what they want or else they wouldn't say that. And here's the thing too. That person's kind of insane for saying that.

It'd be the same as trying to violate a law of physics. If someone came up to you and said, "I'm going to jump 300 meters into the air". You'd be like, "Dude, you're insane that's never going to happen".

Well, these people come up to you and their like, "You would do whatever it takes if you really wanted it badly enough". That statement is just as insane and absurd as someone saying they're going to jump 300 meters into the air.

Why this hasn't been acknowledged or realized? I don't know.

Well, and here's another thing. That person who says that is insane. But some people they'll actually listen to that person. That boss or manager who says, "Do whatever". They'll hear that insanity and then they'll actually listen to that insanity.

So, you've got (exasperation mixed with laughter) …if that conversation was happening inside one person's mind where they got one part of themselves that's saying, "Just do whatever it takes, man", and the other part of their mind says, "OK. OK. You won".

Like, you've got a crazy person, but then the even crazier person is the person who listens to the crazy person.

And so, I don't know what's going on (nervous laughter), but this is happening. And it happens *all* the time.

I think it has to do with people devaluing thoughts as actual things or products.

So, people are kind of prejudice or discriminate against…well, if it's not something I can hold in my hand then it's not important.

Well, that thinking or that mindset has to change because thoughts are just as important as actual physical objects.

Thoughts are things. They attract other things like a physical magnet would. Your thoughts actually create the world around you. They bring things into your world. Thoughts are things.

People make a living. People get paid for their thoughts. That's what comedians do. You know, you have a lot of professions that...psychologists, defense attorneys, self-help teachers...a lot of people...consultants...their product is a thought. And they get compensated for it.

It's very strange that...unless people are in a desperate situation. Like they desperately need to laugh, or desperately self-help, or desperately need a defense lawyer. It's like until they're desperate, they don't want to acknowledge that reality of thoughts and how important and powerful of a product they are and a thing they are.

And that's what I was kind of getting at with this (referring back to article on gardening). I ran across this, "Sure signs a plant needs a bigger pot". And I mentioned shapeshifting (chuckle), but this…I think this actually has a lot of practical application.

So, what happens when a plant grows too big for its pot. So, it says it won't absorb water. It'll tip over. It'll become 'unstable'. You'll also get some damage. It'll actually damage the pot that's too small.

And so, you can actually apply these symptoms to a person that's in an environment that's too restrictive. This is what I was…I talked a little bit about with…when I was telling the story about my eyesight.

So, don't be the pot (laughs). It's fine if the pot grows with the plant. If the pot stays flexible, and it allows progress and it doesn't restrict…so, anyways.

That was a long way off from aliens. Not really though because it's going to come back. It's going to come back to the mind. Which everything is going to come back to.

But these are mental laws. What I'm talking about. And so, you have…and this is going to relate to the stories with the aliens. They're…whatever you believe them to be, they will take on that…thing.

I'm bringing this up because in most of my experiences there's a terrifying aspect. Scary. Traumatic. And it would be very easy to label these encounters or experiences with aliens negative because of how scared you are or how scary it can be.

But that's only if you look at it as a negative. Yeah, that pot that's too small for the plant. That pot is going to look at the plant in a negative way like, "Why are you trying to damage me?"
So, it's how you look at it. And this is…you got the Rorschach ink blot test, right? You ask people to look at this thing and ask them what they see. It really is interesting.

OK. I need to regroup and then we'll get into the story.

Hey guys. So, I'm back. This is another…this is a different day. You can probably see (pointing to desktop calendar) yesterday was the 4th, today is the 5th, Super Bowl Sunday.

I've regrouped. I listened to that first segment of the recording I did, and that got dangerously close to a rant (chuckle) when I was talking about the mental laws.

I do want to say…I do want to say one more thing related to the getting what you concentrate on, and what I was saying about bosses who tell you to do 'whatever it takes'.

Some people might not have ever had someone in their life like that. So, this is a really good movie that really examines these things that I'm talking about. These mental laws.
And actually this is a movie, "Whiplash" from 2014. And you know what…I wouldn't be surprised if…so, this is considered art/movie right now. But in the future, who knows man, this might be like science because once people understand this stuff…it's really…you can do some amazing things with it. Amazing effects in the physical world which is what science and technology does.

The premise of the story for people not familiar. You have a young drummer who wants to be great, and this instructor will stop at nothing. Basically, stops at nothing means he abuses this guy to try to get his full potential out of him.

Right. So, it says…JK Simmons…what it says is…he's trying desperately to find and develop the next jazz legend. So, that's what the teacher wants. At the end. The teacher wants to find and develop the next jazz legend. That's the end.

And so, the student wants to be the next jazz legend. So, we know what both of them want at the end. Each person. The teacher wants to develop greatness and the student wants to be great.

So, I've tried to simplify this. I was telling you how this could work as an equation. So, we know what they both want at the end. They want greatness. Here's the thing.

Like this reviewer mentioned, this guy…the teacher…he's trying to find. Desperately trying to find. So, he's "looking" for greatness. That's what he's doing. And so, what do you think he's going to get at the end? If he's looking for greatness, he's still going to be looking at the end (chuckle). Because that's what he's doing.

How you get greatness. How you find greatness. You actually have to…you actually have to find it…that's what you…you have to accept…you have to accept…you're already great.

You have a saying where people, "fake it until they make it". Somehow these people have…live in a world where the future happens before the present. So, these people fake it…they already…they…I'm going to do probably a separate episode on the emotions and stuff if you've read some of my blog posts…

But, I think that's explained well enough. But it's so simple. I don't know how people get so confused about it. Like this guy (teacher in the movie Whiplash).

You know…and here's the thing…OK, so this is again…we're talking generally here, right? The specifics how of this works. So, if you want greatness at the end, you have to acknowledge that it's already there.

OK. So, where though? Where is this greatness? If it's at the end, people are having trouble seeing it right now. And the reason why is because greatness comes from within. You're not going to find it outside anywhere laying around in the physical world.

It's gonna be…because the physical world…it's all a projection of what's inside…what's inside. So, you gotta look inside and realize that there's greatness…it's already there.

You just gotta get out of the way of it and it will express itself. The problems come when people set up obstacles and abuse and roadblocks and they restrict that greatness. And it comes out in extreme injurious ways like with whiplash and trauma.

So, just get out of the way. You don't need to abuse anyone. Greatness is already there. It's inside of you. It's just very…people like to…people like to make dramatic plays.

I'm not criticizing. I'm just observing and commenting on the mechanics of how these laws work.

So, the greatness it's already there. And here's the thing, or another one of the things about that greatness is that…OK, so what makes something great?

OK. So, this is general (pointing to equation on computer screen). The general is that it's already there. The specifics are that it's inside. It's an inward thing. OK. So, if you're looking for it. It's there already. You don't need to look. It's inside. And it's unique.

That's one of the defining traits of greatness is it's not like anything else. Otherwise, you would just have the thing you already have. It's different. It's new. It's unique.

So, the idea that someone is going to tell you, or instruct you on how to be yourself (giggle), on how to be yourself...that's absurd and ridiculous.

If you want to be unique and yourself...nobody can tell you...nobody can tell you how to be yourself. You just have to practice.

Well, first you have to realize it's there. You have a unique greatness in you and you have to just practice being yourself and it'll come out.

It's hard. It's hard to be yourself. It is. It's a hard thing to do because…you know…that's an entirely different rant…but…I had brought that up and just kind of wanted to put a cap on it. I'm sure it'll come up again because it's such a simple, but controversial thing.

So, the other thing I wanted to cover before I got into the actual meat of the story is…I'm just the…just like with the…I'm…this is how the world is. I'm just the messenger. Don't shoot me. I'm just reporting…I'm just reporting what's out there.

And so, when I get into the alien story here…you know…don't…the world is a strange place. It's stranger, it's curiouser than we can even imagine. So, OK, with that said let me get into the story.

OK. I lied. There was one…there was one last thing that related to these…the mental laws I was just talking about with the boss who says, "Just do whatever it takes", or the abusive instructor we were just talking about with "Whiplash".

So, one of these stories I'm about to tell you. The last person I told this story to he, remarked to me at the end that, you know, I should be careful…I should be careful who I share it with.

So, again this is kind of the same thing we were just talking about. But it's just kind of dressed up in a different disguise. And a lot of things end up being this very simple equation where want you want at the end, you have to be doing all along.

So, this friend that said be careful…be careful who you share that with. He's…in other words he's saying, "Don't be reckless". That there's…you know…that you have to careful of…you have to be careful of a lot of things.

People say that about a lot of things. You have to be careful what you wish for, be careful who you keep company with or be careful who you trust.

So, here's the thing. That mindset, that outlook on life where you're constantly on the lookout, or paranoid or…you know just like what we were just talking about. If that's what you're doing all along as the means, it's very easy to calculate what you're going to have at the end.

At the end you're going to be paranoid and scared. So, while I can appreciate and understand when someone says that…I don't have to blindly obey or implement those thoughts into my…

So, I take that statement, and I reject it. And I've analyzed it. And the thought that I'm going to focus on instead, the thought or the product that we said are real things…I'm not going to focus on the fear or the bad things that will happen…you know what? I'm going to go ahead be and be "reckless".

Because what I want at the end is… I want to be able to express myself freely. And sometimes…sometimes I feel like being reckless. And as long as I'm only being reckless with myself, then I should be able to express that feeling freely.

So, if I want…if at the end I want freedom of expression. Guess what? In our little simple equation…if that's what I want at the end…I'm going to have to express myself freely all along.

It really takes…it takes a little bit of practice to change that mindset where you're…you're really conscious of the thoughts that you're focusing on. That you're putting your energy and your concentration on because you will get…you will get that thing.

If you focus on the fear and the consequences and the danger and the scariness you will get that stuff.

If you choose the thoughts you're going to hold in your head…like your freedom of expression…you know it takes a little bit of practice.

It's a really important thing because…how do you know? People like to assume that, "Yeah, I have freedom. I can do whatever I want." But, go ahead and ty it. Go out…like right now…and express yourself freely. Can you do that? Do you actually have freedom?

If you can't express yourself freely then that's not real freedom. It's something else. Which is another rant entirely.

But this all relates. These are mental laws. And I don't want to be repetitive, but that little trilogy of examples – the do whatever it takes, the abusive teacher, and the freedom of expression – so, it's just…you know…I'm hoping…that's why I'm hoping that the more examples I bring up of each thing that it'll start to get clearer.

Like with the story, how I was saying if it's just 1 or 2 things in your entire life it's kind of hard…those memories…or that…the focus of those thoughts…they kind of get buried in all the other thoughts.

So, yeah, you really got to focus on…

This same concept of thoughts attracting other thoughts…and so, the story I'm going to tell about my most recent…I'm calling alien experience…that…while it was the one singular incident that took place about 3 years ago exactly.

So, if you've read my book I talked about that month, it was March, because I talked about the March Madness basketball tournament that was going on. That whole month was…there was a lot of strange things going on.

But it had gone on…it had gone on…it had built up to that month. Because…after the whole golf venture had collapsed it was…there was…there was strange things that just kind of started building on each other.

And the strange things starting attracting other things. And it kind of culminated in that month where…you just had strange things piling up on top of each other.

So, and it's interesting to me – this is not related to the aliens – this has more to do with free will and how time works and stuff like that. But it…it is…one of the things that it makes me think about with like…especially my life because I've had so many different careers or jobs.

You know…I was in medicine. And then I switched to a completely different job with the playing poker. And then again with screenwriting. And then again with golf…and I'm wondering…it makes you wonder…like how…like if you're born with stuff unconsciously you want to get done.

Right, like there's…like I talked about with my camping trip. There's a vague outline of stuff you want to get done. But the free will part of it is the specifics of how that stuff gets done.

So, if your goal was to shake things up. Just stir up some…discussion…or conversation. I'm thinking the free will is like the specifics of that. Like there's a lot of ways to stir up controversy. You know, you can stir it up in medicine…you can stir it up in…you know… So, I'm just wondering…but anyways. Like I said, there's…that's an entirely…different…

And I also want to, before I get into the recent alien story…and so the first one I feel like it's not…I don't feel like there's a whole lot there other than the missing time because…well, I mean who knows because right now I'm kind of labeling that…I said I've had several experiences.

The first one I remember was…early in childhood. I don't remember how old I was. Somewhere around 5, 6, 7 years old. Somewhere around that age. And I'm labelling it a ghost story.

But who knows because…when people report aliens…they…a lot of times there's grey…there's the grey aliens. But people also report different types of beings. Like glowing beings that were wearing robes with flowing hair, and there's intelligent orbs of energy, there's…the reports of aliens can run the gamut.

So, the one in my childhood…it was just of like a shimmering…a shimmering intelligent thing that appeared in my room. The lights were completely on. I guess I was getting ready for bed or reading or doing something.

And the lights were completely on. This outline of shimmering type material or matter…it appeared near my door. I don't…I don't recall seeing it come through the door. It just materialized.

Obviously, I was a little terrified. Not knowing exactly what it was. And this feeling…is similar to the most recent story because I'm going to talk about how I felt like I had my willpower…my willpower to act or move was…had been shut off or like a kill switch thrown on…

I for sure had that feeling with the recent one. When I was a child…I don't know…well, I remember thinking I probably…I should probably scream for my mommy or something (laughing).
You know…because when I was younger I think my sister never really…she always had problems when she slept. And she would always run into my parents' room and I never… I never really had those problems until this one night…

And its kind of funny because this ties into…kids are always talking about having imaginary friends…not always…but sometimes. Yeah, so I'm wondering…I'm wondering who exactly was messing with my sister (small giggle).

Because I was for sure messed with. And yeah, that's why I'm wondering, "Why didn't I go running for help?" Was I…had a switch been flipped and I was kind of being held there? Because what happened…

So, it appeared near the door. I was in my bed. And the door was near the foot of my bed. So, this thing appeared…I got terrified…those thoughts went through my head, "I wonder if I can scream or go get help?'

But, I didn't say anything. I didn't make any noises. I didn't move. And I was kind of waiting for this thing to like…I guess declare itself or identify itself…who or what is was…some kind of communication…what does it want?

And I guess I found out by its actions. I didn't get any telepathic messages. I was kind of…yeah, I'm sure that was like the main…the main intent that I was broadcasting…like what does it want?

And it responded by…so it was at the foot of the bed by the door where it didn't…it didn't…it came like around the bed. So, I'm thinking…that's why I'm thinking it didn't come through the door. It just kind of materialized because that would have been the shortest route to come get next to me would have been to just come straight up the bed.

But it went around and came up on my left side…and the whole time it was doing this I was thinking, "You know, it still hasn't answered the question. I still don't know what it wants." And it kept getting closer and closer and…

At some point I was like, "Well, I think it wants to get inside my body". Because it was kind of like…enveloping…enveloping me…and then at some point I was like…I think I must have…the thought went through my head that I needed to…I needed to leave.

I needed to like…you know how people talk about going to their happy place when trauma is going on? Well, so yeah, I think I kind of imagined myself in like a…a Disney cartoon…or a Bugs Bunny cartoon or something.

And so, yeah, I just…I lost…I lost consciousness and I went to…I guess…I just dissociated because in my mind I was like, "Well, this thing. I asked it what is wants. It's kind of creep…it's kind of floating or its creeping towards me…and it seems like it wants to get in my body".

And my thinking was, "You can't have two…I'm already in here, right? You can't have two people in one body". So, I was like I guess I need to leave if it wants my body. And so I left. And that's the missing time I was talking about earlier with the Budd Hopkins book.

So, in my mind. I don't know. Who knows? That was…that was the experience I had. And it was a little…it was a little traumatic because I remember for… I don't know for how long afterwards I just remember going to sleep the next night thinking, "Yeah, I wonder if that's going to happen again?"

Even though I don't know what happened because like I said…I lost consciousness. And that's not something…it's not something that I ever actually had a history or habit of doing.

I know some people they faint or they lose consciousness fairly often. It's just like some people get bloody noses. Like that just wasn't a thing. You know I played football. I took a lot of hits to the head. Never really...never had a loss of consciousness like that.

So, on the surface it kind of seems like just a standard ghost story. But it would be interesting to see if maybe there's something more there through regressive hypnosis to look into that missing time.

And I think there's a couple related subjects about that. If you look into the literature where people talk about...where they talk about soul walk-ins. Where someone will walk out of the body, and a new soul will walk-in.

I've heard even people take that concept and they say you could even get like a hybrid soul. Where the one coming in and the one leaving they'll combine or fuse or hybridize...and...I don't...you know...I don't know...it could...so...in my mind...I don't know.

So, that's the first story. So, let me talk about the more recent one. Let me regroup again because I think I went a long...hang on...

OK. I checked the time and this has gotten…this has gotten a little unwieldy already. I think I'm already close to an hour into this, and I just…I've just started getting into the stories.

So, I think…I think I'm just going to go ahead and keep talking and then if I have to chop it up at the end.

I don't know. We'll see how it goes. I did want to make a couple more comments about the last story from my childhood. That I think are pertinent to the other stories.

So, I said I've had several experiences. And so, that first one obviously I was so young. There was no…obviously there was no…psychedelic influence or…

Well, I have had…I did have experiences with other kinds of intelligence on…with psychedelics. Like…Terence McKenna…one of the big ones that talks about…or…he talks about…he talks about machine elves. Self-transforming machine elves.

That he talks about he could see and he interacted with. Not just the elves, I think some of his other books he talks about some interactions with intelligences down in the jungle of the Amazon. With his brother in "True Hallucinations" and "The Invisible Landscape".

Anyways, that experience from when I was a child that was also...you know I had...there was something visually that I was interacting with.

Because some of my other stories...there were effects and you could feel stuff, but you couldn't see anything. But the story from my childhood I could actually see, I told you the shimmering...or the...whatever the space...matter...space-time-matter...whatever this thing it was effecting the atmosphere.

And it's not often that...people don't really talk about...visually. People talk about...when people talk about the "unseen" world and the "spirit" world a lot of times it's just something that's felt, a presence or something.

Not often do you hear people openly talk about seeing things. Seeing manifestations of spirits. This is one of the better books for a lot of reasons "Conversations with Nostradamus"). I've written a couple blog posts about the material in this book.

Some of the other things I like about this book is where Nostradamus talks about...he had spirits visiting him his entire life. That he interacted with and he could visually see in addition to feeling the presence.

And then another good book that people talk openly about these kinds of experiences. This is a good one: "Revelation – The Divine Fire". People sometimes call them ecstatic experiences or enlightenment...or...but they talk about invisible.

So, a lot of people have had visual stuff.

One of the other aspects from the childhood story that I think is interesting that it comes up again with my near death experience. Is that story I was just describing where this thing...this presence...this ghost whatever it was...this entity.

You know, I had thought it was going to want to get inside my body. So, you're talking about 2 things…2 beings occupying the same body. Which is also what I describe in my near death experience at the end of it when I came back from that. And I was occupying 2 bodies.

So, that theme or that concept or that idea. It's kind of been running through my entire life. So, the symbolism there. I'm wondering what it means.

Yeah, I'm going to have to do a probably an analysis of the symbolism after I get done telling these stories. When I get into the explanations and stuff.

I touched on that a little bit with the soul walk-ins and walk-outs and hybrids. But you also have stories about Saints like in the historical past who bi-located. And they were seen in multiple places at once.

And this is an interesting concept because Seth also talks about the concept of an entity or being having more than one body. Seth terms it…he uses the term "counterparts". And I don't have a specific page or book I can refer you to…but he talks about it in several spots.

One of the big things overall. Or one of the big points or messages he tries to get through is we're going to have to really seriously re-evaluate our ideas of what personhood is. And what it looks like…and what it is.

Because we really…our science…for all the things we've examined and looked at and taken apart and experimented with. It's kind of all been outside on objects and things. You know, how far into the Universe we can see, or how small into the atom we can see.

We haven't really looked inward to examine the contents of our mind. I mean we have Psychiatry and….yeah, that's another big issue that I'm probably going to have to deal with in a separate episode.

You also have…talking about our ideas of personhood. You have this multiple personality disorder which is a fascinating condition or phenomenon. And a book that has a good discussion of that is, "The Holographic Universe" by Michael Talbot.

This one (referring to computer screen showing The Holographic Universe). There's a section in there on multiple personality disorder.

I just wanted to point that out really quick. That will probably be covered more in depth in whatever episode that's going to be consciousness or…probably consciousness.

END

Written Transcript from Videocast #5 - Alien Intelligence Part 2

Introduction music

I went ahead and cut off that first episode at around an hour because there's quite a few things I wanted to bring up still concerning that first childhood story.

And it was just going to get too long if I tried to fit that into the first episode because I wanted to try to keep…I wanted to try to keep these things at around an hour maximum.

So, I had brought up…what I'm trying to do right now is just bring up a lot of different angles or ideas or ways to look at the story.

Because when we get into looking at explanations I don't want to discount anything. And I want to be able to draw from as many sources or as many ideas in order to make the explanations make more sense.

So, I'm going to bring up stuff that I feel is related to these stories. So, even if some of those things might not completely match up when we get to the explanation. We might have to take things here and there from different places.

With the first story I had brought up how that theme of 2 people occupying 1 body…or our ideas of personhood. I had brought up multiple personality disorder, and Seth's idea of "counterparts". And bilocation, soul walk-ins and walk-outs.

And so, a couple of the other things…the possibilities that entered into my thinking when trying to understand all this and analyze all this…

I guess one of…one of the funnier…I guess aspects is you always hear…you hear funny stories about people making a deal with the devil. Or selling their soul to the devil for things.

And I've addressed that…the devil…and our symbolism with the devil and our Gods. I've addressed that in one of my blog posts (it's not a blog post yet – but he has written about it on other sites like Reddit) …talking about how we create devils.

When this story happened to me in childhood - like I said I don't remember how old I was 5, 6, 7 – one of the things I do remember very clearly from…probably a little younger than this experience…but I remember I did try to make a deal with the devil when I was…I don't know how old I was.

I was old enough to…I don't even know where I got the concept from. It had to have come from television or cartoons. But I remember being so angry and so upset that…yeah…I really…I was so upset that I was willing to mortgage everything. Everything I had for the power to change my situation.

So, I don't know. They could be unrelated. But who knows? They could be related. And so, I don't want to discount anything. There's a lot of people who do believe forces like that can be harnessed.

And if you look at it as the devil is…look at it as something we create. If you look at it that way. Trying to make a deal with the devil is basically making a deal with yourself. To give yourself the power that you need.

So, that was one of the concepts or the ideas that I haven't fully dismissed.

You know, some people might take that story and run with it. They've seen some of the other things I've done with my eyesight and my near death experience...and they might accuse me of being some kind of dark sorcerer or evil...you know...I'm in league with the devil.

While some people might see me or my story and come to that conclusion, I don't think that's necessarily true.

Because of course you have the saying about...from the bible knowing...being able to tell good and evil by their fruits. And the only person I've ever experimented on or used my powers on is myself so...

It's interesting to examine that angle. I think it's not just interesting...I think it's important to understand...our concepts of Gods and devils.

So, that was another aspect to the story that I think will come up again in the more recent stories.

Also, when I brought up the different types of aliens. I said obviously, there were the greys. Some people report glowing, robed figures with flowing hair. You also have, like I said, the intelligent orbs or sphere of energy.

But then you also have…a lot of people describing Italian looking aliens. Men in Black. John Keel talks about the Mothman. You have the Skinwalker Ranch out in Utah where there's all kinds of different manifestations of energy.

So, yeah, the aliens can really run the gamut. I'm not sure what quite to call that story yet. Alien, ghost. So, it's just a story.

Another aspect I think is interesting is how I brought up how my sister also had some issues with sleeping while growing up. And one of the other aspects about alien encounters or alien abductions. A lot times people report having a history of being abducted throughout their entire lives.

And not only being personally abducted from a young age. But also some people report their entire families have been in contact since they were young.

Also, I've heard stories where it runs it families. Where the parents have experiences, the children will also have experiences.

And so, I definitely had stuff happen to me. From my observations, my sister had stuff happen to me (he meant to say "my sister had stuff happen to *her* - this might be a synchronicity though since it was 9:22 into the recording and that's my birthday – Sep 22).

She says, I asked her about it recently. I said, "Do you remember anything unusual from childhood?" Because I remember she was always running into my parents' room, but she doesn't recall anything specifically.

But if you keep in mind that the aliens can shut down people…shut down their willpower. They can shut down automobiles. They can make people forget certain…forget certain things. Screen memories. Talked about in that "Communion" book I mentioned earlier. A lot of times with animals. Screen memories with animals. Owls and deer.

So, I had experiences. *I* think my sister did. You know, my parents were always kind of weird too. So, (chuckling) who knows if they were born weird or they were also having experiences.

So, I'm not ruling out that aspect. I think it's important to take into consideration at least. And one of the other things that passed through my mind while thinking about all this stuff…

You know with my parents being weird…I didn't rule out that they might have had something to do with that experiment (he misspoke again and said experiment instead of experience). They were conducting some type of ritual possibly…uh black magic rituals…while the children were sleeping.

Whether what I saw was one of their…one of their creations. Or was it a side effect of some…some darker magic…or some black magic…that they were doing on their own.

And how I talked about with certain types of thoughts attracting similar thoughts and thoughtforms. So, you know, if they were doing…if they had any…practice…where they were…trying to…harness or…use…some forces like that.

It wouldn't be too much of a stretch that other similar dark forces were being attracted. We also had…we had a bunch of weird…some weird issues with our phone. Where we would keep getting calls.

A lot people report that with aliens too. Is that they'll get calls with hang ups or weird messages. We did have issues with our phone.

And it's not that far out there when you talk about black magic or just even suspecting or having suspicions your parents might be into that.

Because not only were my parents a little weird, but we... I grew up in Clearwater, FL. Which is the headquarters of the religion of Scientology.

And L Ron Hubbard, the founder of Scientology, his son...Ron DeWolf? Yeah, Ronald DeWolf. Hubbard's son. He...died under suspicious circumstances...(mumbling)...diabetes complications.

He commented to...so DeWolf claimed that "Black magic is the inner core of Scientology. Arguing my father did not worship Satan. He thought he was Satan."

And so Hubbard had connections to Aleister Crowley and also...Jack Parsons of JPL, jet propulsion labs. That's another...I'll probably have to do another episode on that because...I have actually looked a lot into Scientology.

Like I said, I grew up in Clearwater, FL which is the headquarters of Scientology. My parents were a little weird. And there's also a couple of other coincidences between...my parents and Scientology because my dad actually worked for the IRS as a special field agent.

And this was in the early 70's when my father worked for the IRS and...Scientology has a long history with the IRS. If you want to look into Operation Snow White.

This was the Church of Scientology's internal name for a major criminal conspiracy during the 70's. One of their...so...this is actually pretty insane...if you look...if you look at the details of this.

So, they infiltrated 136 government agencies, foreign embassies, consulates in more than 30 countries. One of the largest infiltrations...one of the largest! It has to be THE largest? 5,000 covert agents!

That's amazing…yeah…that…what did it say? Major criminal conspiracy! Well, and here's the thing. 136 government agencies in 30 countries 5,000 agents…but here's the thing is that only…only 12 people got…punished or held responsible for this.

So, that leaves 4,988…um spies…who got away scot free. And it's interesting to speculate with my father who was…who worked for the IRS. So, yeah, my father worked for the IRS in the early…he worked for the IRS…I think he worked for them while this Operation was going on.

So, you gotta wonder if any of those 5,000 agents…whether those were people who already worked for the government and Scientology was able to flip them? You know, I'm sure they had some of their own home grown agents, but I'm sure they did recruiting.

And it's also interesting is that right after this. I think this was 1974 or 1975. But right after that my dad…no longer worked for the IRS. He went into private practice. And that's when we actually moved to Clearwater, FL.

We had lived in Chicago when…when…so, it's strange, yeah. During this Operation he was with the IRS. After this happened he left. And where he went to was Clearwater, FL the headquarters…the international headquarters of Scientology.

So, you gotta wonder. If they're recruiting people who already work for the IRS. They need them to do stuff. They promise them, "Hey, help us out with this Operation. And afterwards come down to Clearwater and we'll help you setup your own private accounting business. We can promise you clients from Scientology."

And the other interesting thing…there's a lot of coincidences with my family and Scientology. One of Scientology's symbols is the pyramid. And when my dad moved to Clearwater and started his CPA business…he had a triangle on his business card.

So, I've done a lot of reading about Scientology. I might do, like I said, I might do a separate episode on that. Maybe make it part of a larger episode about religion in general.

Yeah, I think the symbolism of that first story is interesting too. Like I said the symbolism with the multiple bodies or the multiple people in one body. But also the shimmering mass of indefinite or undefined mass...or this vague ghostly thing like...I think there's some interesting symbolism there too.

There was one more thing about the first episode...I need to regroup again hang on.

OK. Well, I can't remember that last thing I wanted to say about the childhood story.
So, I'm just going to go ahead and move forward to some of the other ones. I had talked about this a little bit already.

How some of my more recent stories they started...they started to build on each other. After the golf fell apart. There was...strange things started attracting other strange things and they started building and...

There was just a whole...the whole month of March was just a very strange month. In the beginning of the month what happened was. I was getting a lot of...I was getting a lot of synchronicities...

I don't know if people are familiar with synchronicities. But it's just…an acausal connecting principle. So, this is from Carl Jung. You can find some of his books on my website. He has a lot of academic work that's got a lot of technical jargon that's not very accessible to the majority of people.

But he also has several books that are meant for the layperson. And so those are a few of them (referring to website).

One of his big…one of Carl Jung's big concepts was this synchronicity. Acausal. So, he's saying things are connected. But it doesn't appear that way. There doesn't…or we can't yet understand how and why they're connected, but they are connected.
So, I was getting a lot of those. A lot of those symbols that seem to be connecting with not a lot of rhyme or reason. Conscious rhyme or reason.

And I was also doing…and so in that month I was also doing a lot of experiments with remote viewing. Which it's…that's a military term. Remote viewing that's military jargon for psychic abilities, extra sensory perception.

There's also some books you can check out on that. That book. This book, Ingo Swann. He's considered the father of remote viewing.

What he did...he's the one that designed the protocols. I think he's the one that came up with the term. So, Ingo Swann he was just...not just...he was an artist and a psychic living in New York and the government got into studying him and trying to weaponize...trying to weaponize psychics (chuckle).

That's a real interesting area to look into. I'll probably do another episode on that like all the other things I was talking about.

So, during this month. I was getting a lot of synchronicities. I was experimenting with remote viewing. I was having several smaller out of body experiences before I had the near death experience later in the month.

Robert Monroe talks a lot about out of body journeys. He's got a trilogy of books. "Journeys Out of the Body", "Far Journeys" and "Ultimate Journeys". He...Robert Monroe also...he was also working with the government and the military with remote viewing like Ingo Swann was.

And there's actually...there's a Monroe Institute in...I think Virginia. And the government was...so, Ingo Swann came up with the protocols. And then for further training the government was sending remote viewers, or psychics, to the Monroe Institute where they were learning how to explore consciousness.

You can look into that. Robert Monroe...also he went to visit Jane Roberts. The woman who channeled the Seth Material. So, you know there's psychic communities. Just like there's communities for other...other interests and fields...you know you have sailing communities...so there's...

And so these people...and I think that's what Monroe. That's what I like about his first book. Is that when this stuff first started happening to him he was just as confused as I felt I was.

So, he went looking for explanations and he was talking with all kinds of people. And one of the people he went to see was Jane Roberts.

So, that month. I was having synchronicities. Experimenting with remote viewing. And having some smaller out of bodies.

And my near death experience actually happened. It happened a week after…actually that month I had two alien encounters. Well, the whole month was kind of weird.

I was…I did get several messages…that I don't know where they came from. But as far as stuff that fit the textbook…fit the textbook…what people describe with aliens. One of them was strictly telepathic.

The…I guess the big dramatic story with the aliens. That happened a week before my near death experience. And then the telepathic incident I wanna say happened a week after the NDE. So, there's like 3 weeks there.

But at the beginning of the month I was doing all this fringe experimentation…one of the other things I wanted to bring up while I'm bringing up the out of bodies and remote viewing and all that stuff is…

We were talking about connecting principles. A lot of the people associated with the remote viewing project…like I mentioned Ingo Swann…a lot of the remote viewers or psychics actually had a background of Scientology. Either before they started working with remote viewing or afterwards.

And yeah, Scientology has had a lot of fights going on with the IRS. But they also...they're claiming...Scientology is claiming that remote viewing and a lot of these psychic technologies are copyrighted Scientology technologies being illegally utilized by the United States Intelligence.

So, they've filed years and years of legal complaints.

So, you can look into that. Yeah, you have to wonder...it makes you wonder what the government's response to Operation Snow White was.

Because there's always going to be blowback. With anything. With anything that's done. But especially you're going to get blowback...I think that's actually a CIA term, blowback?

Yeah, blowback. Originated in the intelligence community. Unintended consequences. So, yeah you have Scientology infiltrating the government, the US government, IRS. Yeah, like it said, 30? 30 countries.

That's insane. So, you gotta wonder what the blowback was. So, Scientology infiltrates the government. The government is probably going to do something in return. And I think that's what this is talking about, this article (Federal Cover-Up of Scientology in Military Intel).

I think what it's saying is that…so, Scientology infiltrated the US government. And then the US government, specifically the NSA – I think, counter-infiltrated. Stole these technologies and is keeping the copyrights? You know, it's such a mess. I guess you could go down that rabbit hole forever.

But I just wanted to bring that up because a lot of these things are related.

Anyways. So, the other thing I did want to point out is that there's a lot of fantastical elements to the stories that happened in that month of March.

And so, the big dramatic one involves levitation, telepathy, shapeshifting. I also had telepathy in the one that happened a couple weeks later.

If you remember all the way back to the first episode I claimed that my near death experience was the most incredible thing that happened to me. And the reason I claimed that, my near death experience, instead of this alien where I was levitating and shapeshifting is because I'm absolutely certain I caused, or I induced, the near death experience.

I think that's just…people like to feel…or people feel…if they're the author or creator of it I think they favor those experiences that they've created. And I don't know…I don't know exactly who was responsible for the alien incident.

It's possible…. like I think I mentioned before…it's how you look at it. It's possible that whatever those forces were they could be a larger aspect of myself that was trying to send myself a message.

I'm going to analyze that a little bit after the story. So, I just wanted to point that out. The reason for why I was claiming the near death experience was the most incredible. Even though levitation and shapeshifting are pretty incredible as well.

It's…yeah, it's possible I was responsible. Or my larger self was responsible for those experiences. And I do want to get into…I do want to get into that concept or that idea about how we could be responsible for a lot of stuff.

Going back to how I said if you have a terrible boss or manager who tells you, "Do whatever it takes". An interesting way to look at that would be…you know, is that boss or manager, is that actually…is that actually someone else?

Could that possibly be a part of me that's testing me or giving me a message to see what I do with it?

And that goes back to our ideas of personhood. It's possible that…I think Seth gets into…I don't know if I've done a blog post on this specifically, but when he talks about that concept of "counterparts".

He brings up that Jesus or Christ. The Christ entity or being. He was saying that Jesus, that Christ was actually…he was John the Baptist, Jesus and Paul or Saul of Tarsus. He was all 3 of those people at the same time.

Because those 3 people's lives overlapped. I think in total they spanned 100 years or so, but there was also overlap there. And I think...if I'm remembering correctly. I'll have to go back and find the exact Seth...the citation.

But I think he was saying that not only was Christ: John the Baptist, Jesus and Paul but he was also the 12 disciples. I think he was saying those were fragments of the Christ personality.

So, he was saying Christ had these 15 personalities. At least. That we know of. Or that Seth points out. And so Christ just kind of put on this really huge dramatic...play. That is still being talked about thousands of years later.

We could get deep into the multiple person stuff. Let me get to the story though.

So, the month was getting strange. What was happening was. I was getting all these synchronicities. I was doing out of body, remote viewing. OK. So, what had happened was I went over to my friend's house one night...

The reason I went over there was, I told you I was getting some synchronicities. One of them was suggesting that I contact my friend and get a hold of him.

And so, I went over to his house the one night. We talked for a bit. I told him some of the strange stuff that was going on that month and it got...we talked for a little while. About weird stuff.

What I thought at the time was weird stuff. Because when I went to leave it went a whole 'nother dimension of weirdness.

We were talking. And then I went out to my car. Just as I got in the driver's seat to leave I started getting...I started feeling...I started getting a strange feeling.

The way I can describe it now after I've done a lot of reading is...what I was talking about earlier where I felt like I lost my willpower. My ability to act. And to do what I wanted.

At the time I didn't know what was going on. I had gotten into my car and was wanting to go home. But I couldn't...I couldn't summon my body to do what I wanted.

And like I said back to the childhood experience. Similar to that. Where the thoughts that went through my head as a child were, "I should yell. I should run." But I didn't do anything.

This time I didn't do anything. But at first I wasn't terrified. I wasn't scared. Not at first.

So, I was just sitting there and I was wondering, "OK. This is a weird feeling". Then…and then what happened is that's when I started levitating. So, I was sitting in my driver's seat and something was lifting me up.

It lifted me up. It was gradual. I think it brought me up…it brought me up…I think I actually hit the ceiling of the car with my head. And I came back down and I think I was just kind of hovering between the seat and the ceiling.

Which is interesting because a lot of times when people report abductions they say went through a window…or the beam…they could go through objects.

So, I wasn't aware of any of the alien or UFO literature when this was happening. Right now, I have the benefit of a lot of literature and reading that I've done to help analyze.

But at the time I had no clue. No clue. I thought I was…well, the levitation I thought was pretty darn cool (laughing). Because while it was happening, I was sitting in my car in front of my friend's house.

And I looked…I looked over to the house because I wanted to get my friends attention and be like, "Dude, look I'm levitating out here!" There was…I couldn't…there was nothing…I couldn't get anyone's attention.

I looked across the street to the neighbor's house…it was almost eerily…eerily quiet. And now that I have a better viewpoint of it, I'm wondering if…you know, how they can…maybe how they made my sister forget stuff or…you know, they can…

So, I'm wondering…I'm sure…after I describe the rest of it…they have…whoever it was…had to have control over the entire area…

Because what happened was I lost my willpower. Someone started levitating me. And I was like, "This is pretty cool". And then what happened was…

I felt a beam. Like a beam of energy from above. Came down focused on my head. But it didn't...not quite...not like my physical skull or my body.

It was...it was like this beam was going through...through my skull...not into my brain...but into my mind.

And what it felt like it was doing was. To me it felt like it was collecting, or it was gathering my thoughts. Like 35 years of...40 years of my thinking and stuff. It felt like they were gathering all of that stuff. And uploading it from my mind. While it was happening I remember...I remember wondering why it was taking so long.

I guess probably the beam lasted for maybe...somewhere around 5 or 10 minutes. Cause after a certain point...this was all...it was still fairly benign up to this point.

You know, I lost my willpower. I was levitating. And then this beam came down...and I'm...and you know I'm not a big privacy person. You know, I'm pretty much an open book.

So, it didn't bother me that someone wanted to take a look at (small giggle) everything I've ever thought.

And so…and so I was wondering why it was taking so long. But then when I started thinking about it I was like, "Yeah. OK. Well, I guess 40 years' worth of stuff in 5 minutes. That's…that's pretty good compression technology." (laughter)

This beam I'm talking about. It's not…I'm not the only one who's described something like that.

You have David Icke. I don't know how you say his name. Icke? Icke (different pronunciation)?
His story from Peru that he talks about. Near Lake Titicaca. He describes it as, "A flow of powerful energy began to go into the top of my head like a drill. And I could feel the flow going the other way up from the ground up through my feet."

And so he says…and then the voice said very clearly, "It will be over when you feel the rain".

And so this went on for…he says his feet continue to burn and vibrate for 24 hours. The actual beam though…well over an hour.

OK. So, I had the beam for 5 or 10 minutes. And I didn't feel anything in my feet because I was levitating. And the beam wasn't going into...well, it was in...it was into my head, but it felt like it was pulling stuff out.

This...this statement. "It will be over when you feel the rain".

Now...like...I brought up earlier how I had some weird messages I don't know where they came from. I'll get back to those later though. The messages. Because it didn't happen at the time.

More with the beam. This is...actually...this David Icke story. He also talks about shapeshifting. Shapeshifting reptiles.
I haven't got too far into his work to know exactly how he came up with that theory. Or what exactly he means by that theory. But my experience also had shapeshifting reptiles.

Sammy Hagar. When he was younger...I guess he had multiple. So, 1967 and 1951. This is what I was getting at with people talking about having lifelong encounters.

So, this was on Howard Stern he was talking about this stuff. He talked about being hooked up to something as well. He wasn't sure if it was...he wasn't sure if it was uploading or downloading information.

I didn't feel like it was downloading. It kind of sound like...David Icke sound like...I don't know. It might have been both. But Hagar says..."or if they were uploading out of my head or to see what I knew. Like an experiment".

OK. So, I'm not by far the only person to talk about aliens or even beams into the head.

So, this is where...this is where it kind of takes a really strange turn.

If losing your willpower and levitating and having 40 years of your thoughts collected with an energy beam in 5 minutes. If that's weird enough, what happened next was the shapeshifting.
And I wasn't quite ready for...I wasn't...I wasn't quite ready for what happened next because I had...I thought the encounter was over at that point.

I was kind of distracted. I thought, "OK. They shut me down. They showed me a cool trick. And they took some stuff. And I guess I can go on my way now. I can hit the road."

And so I was a little distracted waiting for them to finish. Like I said I was a little impatient. Yeah, and I think the symbolism is interesting there too with me wanting to know, "Why is this taking so long?"

More with the time aspect. Like the symbolism with time. How I brought up in one of the blog posts about aliens. How a lot of times when people have encounters with aliens they talk about the aliens asking, "What time is it?"

And I don't think they're quite asking so much as telling. Giving messages. About aspects of our world and reality.

So, there's the symbolism with time and so I was wondering, "What's taking so long?" I was getting ready…and the next…I'm still levitating…when the beam was done…I was still levitating…

What I noticed next because it caught me off guard was my body. I noticed my body doing weird things.

I kind of stopped paying attention to my body a little bit I guess because I couldn't move it.

What I noticed next was my body was kind of like…it was doing stuff on its own.

And it was…what it felt like was my jaw was almost like trying to unhinge itself. Like when you see snakes trying to swallow or digest something large and their jaws will unhinge.

That's what I felt like my jaw was trying to do…and it was like my tongue…my tongue was trying to get like outside my body.

Like you know how snakes stick out their tongue? I showed that article about how they do that to get a sense of their surroundings.

So, my jaw was trying to unhinge My tongue was trying to get as far outside of my body as possible.

And also what was happening was…so this is kind of the reptilian stuff…and so…that was my actual physical body – my jaw and my tongue.

But also, that was my physical body. I felt like my energy body was also shapeshifting. Like the astral body or the energy body.

Especially around my head area. It felt like my head was changing. It was changing almost into a reptilian head or a serpent head. Where your eyes are kind of…on the sides of your head. Like a bird or a fish.

And so my vision was getting a little wacky. And…you know my head…it was changing shape, but it also felt like it was also getting a little bigger.

So, (deep sigh). What to make of that symbolism? Because…Icke. I think David Icke…he doesn't…like I said…I don't know enough about his reptilian theory. What I think I know about it is that…the reptilians are bad.

But I was a reptile in this story (chuckle). Well, and here's one of the things I'm wondering at with the symbolism. Well, they uploaded…I felt they uploaded with the beam.

And I'm wondering if they took all that data or thoughts or energy. That was what they took. And then I'm wondering…if then they were…they were going to give me stuff.

So, they took stuff with the beam. And then maybe they were giving me stuff.

Kind of like how Hagar wondered whether they were uploading or downloading.
So, maybe with me they uploaded…they uploaded with the beam. But then to give me information they did it in a more creative and symbolic ways.

So, I'm wondering if the…if the…me turning into the reptile was…maybe they looked into my future? Well, so they took my thoughts. 40 years of my thoughts with the beam. And then they could…they could also see…how things might…how things would play out?

And maybe they saw me becoming the Fire Snake? And it's possible with the levitation that they also saw…that they also saw me looking into gravity? But that…the levitation actually happened before they used the energy beam. So, I don't know with that.

One of the other interesting things with symbolism. And the reptilian. That we talked about the other day. With Paul the Apostle.

When we…when I…was going over his conversion experience. And I thought about this after that podcast where it said that when his vision healed…that…I can't find it…someone must have taken it out…I can't find it. Interesting.

But it had said…I guess I could go back to the old podcast. But it said that, "The scales fell out of his eyes".

And I was wondering if that was symbolic. Not…at the time I was kind of jokingly saying scales because we were looking at the snakes…how they can boost their eyesight.

But I'm wondering if scales meant symbolism for…like the scales fell out of Pauls' eyes. Like he…so he no longer…like the scales of justice…so he was no longer going to judge people.

Because I think Paul was…Paul was very…he was militant. In his approach. Zealous. And so he attacked I think. He attacked a lot of the Christians. Until…this event.

So, maybe the scales falling out of his eyes meant that he was no longer…he was not going to judge and attack people…look at things without…

I thought that was interesting to bring up. So, back to…back to…what happened…

So, the…yeah. I got my willpower knocked out. Started levitating. They used the beam. I turned into a reptile.

And so this distortion with my…with my head. Where I felt…where my vision was messed up. And it felt like I had a serpent head.

That lasted for…that lasted till I drove home. From my friend's house. Which was a good…couple hours later. And that kind of fits in with David Icke story where he says, "still 24 hours later".

So, I was still having effects from this encounter hours later at home. Not just with the shapeshifting, but with the…one of the other things I'll get to in a second.

Well, here's what I was wondering too…as far as the symbolism with the reptilian symbolism. Yeah, I…it's also possible…I was speculating maybe they looked into my future.

Is it possible…is it possible that…because I couldn't see anything. Because I couldn't see who was doing this to me. That was my way of…like the snakes stick out their tongue to get a sense of their surroundings.

Was that a way for me to try to figure out who was doing this to me? Was my astral body or my energy body doing the sensing or the perceiving for me because I couldn't see these things?

So, it was…I'm wondering if it was maybe…these forces were radiating a certain energy. And that energy was causing me to shift into something similar to what they were?

The other thought I had as far as the reptilian symbolism too was with…so from here on out it turned into…for me at the at the time it turned into like a battle.

It was like a battle for my soul. So, I was…one of the other speculations that I had was. Was that me trying to prepare, or get ready, for what was to follow? The assault. And I was calling on maybe…I sensed the power of what was interacting with me…and maybe I was calling on that ancient…that ancient DNA?

The dinosaur DNA. And those memories. And I was calling upon that for strength in the battle with whatever I was about to interact with?

And that's where I was talking about that "Altered States". In that movie they get into…they talk about shapeshifting back towards…back towards…primitive man.

Maybe I shifted all the way back, past man, past whatever to…ancient reptilian serpents or whatever? I don't know.

Well, OK. So, yeah, what happened next was the battle. And…

How I describe it is…I'm still there…levitating. But I've shifted into some type of reptile/serpent and…

What happened next was this thing…it felt like it was in front of me. And what it did was…it reached inside of me. Kind of like it did with the energy beam into my head.

But not into my brain. Like I said. The beam went into my mind. And my thoughts. Not anything physical like my brain.

This thing reached inside of me, but not to grab my intestines. But it grabbed my spirit. And my...the core of me.

And it tried to pull...it tried to pull it out. Pulled it up...you know like I said...I was levitating and I was halfway between the driver's seat and ceiling. But it felt when this thing was pulling...trying to pull my spirit out...it was pulling like up out of the car.

Like a good 10 feet or so. And it felt like my spirit was just attached by the *tiniest* thread. And I was like holding on with all my...all the might I could muster.

At the time I described it as agony. Because it did that once. For about...I want to say 15 or 20 seconds. And you just...absolutely every ounce of strength I could summon. To keep some connection with my body.

It did it once. And then it...like a rubber band...it kind of...the tension released. And it came back. But then it did it again. Like 2 or 3...

So, after the...after the 3rd or 4th time of this. Where...and each time it pulled until there was like the tiniest...tiniest...it felt like the tiniest thread connecting me.

After like the 4th time or so…I got…I got the feeling that…actually I laughed to myself about it at the time...and I started thinking like, "I guess we can do this all night".

I had resigned myself (chuckle) to the fact that whatever this thing was. It was just going to torture me regardless of how I felt about it.

And I was thinking too…with how I commented about the beam like, "Why is this taking so long? Are we done yet?"

And I felt that same way when it was trying to pull me out. I got the feeling that…OK…I felt that…whatever this thing was it was way more powerful than me.

If it could levitate me, if it could shapeshift me, and it could…I'm sure…if it really wanted to it could have ripped me entirely out. And so…

I don't know. I thought, "Yeah, I guess we can do this all night". In like a humorous way.

And I don't think this thing really cared. You know, it did it a couple more times. And yeah, at the time…it was agony.

Also at the time…so when it was finished. At the time, I got the feeling that it might have been a little angry that it couldn't…that it couldn't completely get me out.

So, what it did then was. It hit me with like a lightning bolt of energy. That staggered me for hours.

The ripping out with my soul. That didn't linger. That would go on for like I said 15 or 20 seconds. But when it was over it didn't really linger. Until they did it again.

But this lightning bolt. The quality of the pain. It was like…it reverberated…just…like…very similar to what Icke said about, "burning and vibrating".

I wouldn't say like actual…heat burning. But just energy burning. Yeah, so when I got back to my house a couple hours later I was staggered.

I felt like I had gotten into a fight with Mike Tyson or something (laughing).

And so, yeah, it hit me with that lightning bolt. It went…it went like diagonally through my body. Starting from…like my heart area.

It went diagonally down to the right. And yeah. That hurt. (laughing?)

I mean, you know, the soul ripping hurt too. But... What happened after that was...so, this is when I got one of the telepathic messages.

So, onto each of my eyes. So, onto one eye...at the same time...it projected an image onto each of my eyes.

On the right eye...so, this was at the same time...on the right eye it was like a symbol of an angel. And then on the left eye it transmitted an image of a demon.

So, an angel on one eye and a demon on the other. And at the time how I interpreted that. I thought this thing...I thought this thing had...evaluated or judged...my soul or my spirit.

It had looked with the beam. And then it had taken a look...a closer look without the technology. Just kind of ripping it out and looking around.

I got the feeling it didn't like what it saw (chuckle). So, that's why it hit me with the lightning bolt.

And then it was saying, "Well, you're not all bad though…" That was how I interpreted it at the time.

As an attack. I've come to adjust that thinking though. Let me…OK so…

It projected these images and…I had thought it was just the one…the one thing in front of me. That was doing all this stuff to me.

And possibly maybe the energy beam was coming from a UFO higher up in the…in the sky.

But I guess what I found out was…that I was surrounded. Because then I started getting like astral punches thrown at me.

After the thing in front of me had finished. Because these punches started coming from the sides.

And yeah. So, I told you I felt like I had gotten in a fight with Mike Tyson. I was trying to…somehow I summoned the energy to get home.

Along the way…they got…they kept throwing…they kept wailing on me. The drive home. I didn't know if I was going to make it.

It felt like they might even have been trying to…trying to get me lost. Trying to…who knows.

I think this is getting the…near the end of the 2nd episode. So, let me see if I can summarize this at a good point. Where we can continue in the next episode.

So, I think that's a good way to look at. At the time I didn't have a clue. And a lot of things were happening to me during that month that were new and strange.

And so this was a new and strange…and at the time I looked at it as negative. I thought…I thought that someone was angry with me.

Someone was trying to…well, I also took that lightning bolt as a warning. That…don't say anything about this because we have to power to just…to zap you.

The more I read about this kind of stuff after the event…that is something people report with aliens. Where they do say stuff like that. Like, "Don't talk about this. Don't tell anyone. Or else…something bad will happen".

But with those stories…what those people…people who eventually do end up talking. They say that nothing actually happened to them. So…

And that relates to what I was saying at the very beginning of segment with the friend who I told you advised that I should, "Be careful who I share this with." And don't be reckless.

It's a very similar type of thinking…that I myself was having at the time. I was thinking, "I don't know if I should be talking about this…or sharing this." Because that could be interpreted as a warning.

But now that I have more distance or perspective and…some knowledge to better assess…I've taken…well, at first…I didn't even want to attribute it to aliens.

At first I thought these are humans…these were like…powerful dark wizards or sorcerers that were…they had grouped up…and attacked me for whatever reason. I don't know.

And I'm not dismissing that either. So, if anybody thinks that this…humans could do this. I'm willing to listen.

From what I can tell…this is not stuff that humans can do. I know Dr. Steven Greer…he does talk about where he thinks some of the abductions have been stage by our own government.

And I think one of the specific examples of that…there was a politician…an ambassador…to the UN. From Guam I think? I think he was the Secretary General of the UN?

Yeah, here it is. This was in the middle of Manhattan. And that had some interesting political timing.

Because this gentleman…yeah, Dr. Steven Greer is saying, "This was a false flag abduction".

And so, yeah, one of those books on my website talks about that event. But it doesn't talk about Dr. Greer's analysis.

This book (UFOs and the National Security State: The Cover Up Exposed 1973-1991). I think it's in that 2nd volume. Yeah, if it's 1989. That story is in that book.

And so, OK. But even if…even if humans could do all that. That's not…that's not completely human technology their using though.

They gotta be getting that technology from actual aliens. Like, you know, reverse engineered.

Like they talk about in…"The Day After Roswell". And I talk about…a little bit in some of my blog posts.

So, that was my initial thought. I was like…." Humans are mad at me."

And then…so my thinking changed to…" I don't think humans can do this." Not alone.

So, there's gotta be some type of aliens involved. And so, that's where my thinking went for a little while…I was still looking at it as negative.

Now, I'm kind of looking at it like…I was talking about earlier with…and I talk about in some of…my blog posts. About how these aliens could possibly be…us. From the…future.

So…not even from the future. It could just be a larger…a larger aspect of…your own self.

Yeah. OK. But. Then so, the other…there was one more. The strictly telepathic incident.

Well, OK. Here's why…here's why I'm wondering…yeah, I think I might cut it off here and then start up a new episode.

END

Written Transcript from Videocast #6 - Alien Intelligence Part 3

Hello there everyone and welcome to Episode 6. This will be the 3rd Part of the Alien Intelligence Trilogy.

So, if you remember from the last episode…near the end of that I had kind of finished up telling one of my stories from the month of March. And I had started to look at the symbolism a little bit with that story.

And I want to continue to look at the symbolism. A little bit more. So, I'm giving you my outline here for this episode or this 3rd part of the series.

So, what I want to try to cover today. I want to finish up the aliens because I'm getting a little burnt out on them and I'm sure you guys are too.

So, I want to finish that up. Move on to some other stuff. And then probably do another series of alien episodes. Probably do another trilogy in the future focusing around some of the blog posts I've done.

So, to wrap up in this episode…what I want to cover is…I want to get a little more into the symbolism of that one story.

I want to tell a couple of the other stories. And then I want to look at the symbolism of those other stories as well.

And then also, I always try to leave room for random stuff that'll pop up along the way.

So, that's what I'm looking to get done here today.

One of the things I wanted to start talking about in this episode before I get back into the aliens.

Is that…there's…well, the reason I'm going to bring stuff up like this is…I'm usually only going to bring up stuff that seems unrelated.

But I'm either going to…or I've already either brought it up and talked about it and it's related, or I'm going to bring it up in the future.

So, while it might not seem to be talking about aliens here, but this is an important concept I think because I had brought up a little bit with talking about our ideas of personhood.

And the whole story with Christ and how he had multiple personalities all at the same time. And the effect of that was...a big dramatic story. That...it served a lot of purposes.

So, and one of the other things I've been talking about a lot recently too is emotions.

And how people...how our...how our society and our current civilization likes to downplay emotions. Or give them a lesser position in whatever hierarchy...

So, people are real focused on intellectual, logical, rational understanding of the world.

But there's also an emotional understanding as well. An intuitive understanding that's just as important.

And that's why I've been trying to bring up several...several angles or ways to look at things and stories. You know emotional understanding, intellectual understanding, symbolic understanding. And within each of those you can have many different ways to look at the symbolism.

So, when you're talking about drama. And its purposes. And what it can do.

If you look back, all the way back to the myths of old. The religions of old. You had famous story tellers...you know Homer and...

It's just the history of humans is filled with stories.

And I think it's important to understand...not just that drama...drama and emotions and intuition...not just that their important. But I want to try to get a little bit into the mechanics of how drama works. Just like I've tried to give a little bit of the mechanics behind how...I talked about a little with sports. And like golf and the mechanics with some of the mental approach to that.

I think I also mentioned I was going to get into a little bit of the mechanics with poker so...

These are just the mechanics as I understand them.

Maybe it will help someone else.

So, what I can tell you about drama. Because I did...I did spend a few years writing screenplays. Learning how to write screenplays.

How to create stories that are…resonate and people connect with.

And so there…there does appear to be structure. Or certain principles. Like I said mental laws.

So, if you want to take that a little bit further and relate it to our stories. We can try to look at the structure. And see what's there.

So, the structure…as an example that's right in our minds. The way that I'm structuring these episodes.

So, this is part 3 of the Alien Intelligence. And so, this is a little trilogy.
And I said I wanted to come back to aliens. And I kind of have a trilogy of blog posts. That I want to get back to. I might make that a separate trilogy.

But this concept of a trilogy is how…is how a lot of people learn to understand drama.

And I did talk about this a little bit already in the 2nd episode with my…with the story of eyesight and how it healed – my Miraculous Healing.

And I…while I was telling the story I kind of dropped hints that there were three parts to the story. A beginning, a middle, and an end. And so, this is kind of the structure that drama takes.

There's…they talk about…OK…you're going to have to really bear with me because I'm a terrible drawer. But I'm going to try to…I'm going to try to give a visual of how…

Let's see…OK…whoops…alright. So, you have a line. A fairly straight line. And so you have 3 parts. You have…right? You have a beginning, a middle (laughing at terrible artwork), and an end.

So, this would be the beginning. Oops. Beginning…alright this is terrible.

Let me start over with this. OK.

OK. So, I'm going to try to…I'm going to try to show this in Photoshop instead of MS Paint because I have a little more familiarity with this program.

But anyways. So, there's these 3 parts. You've got a beginning, a middle, and an end.

And how a lot of this works is…you might even see a lot of people complaining about how modern movies are real formulaic.

Well, there's a reason why. Because and so this is a little bit of the formula that's used.

And a lot of this formula comes from this book I was spotlighting a second ago "The Hero's Journey" by Joseph Campbell. And he did a lot of studying into myths and archetypes.

A lot of the same stuff Carl Jung delved into. So, there's a lot of…he gets into a lot of myths and mystical understanding, magickal understanding.

And so this is one of the good books I haven't put up on my website yet ("The Hero's Journey).

And then this same principle. This 3-Act Structure. It's also…it's used all the time in Hollywood. Hollywood movies.

It's used in politics because you've got…I don't know if people are familiar with…well, here's another good book that I haven't put up yet – "The Shock Doctrine" by Naomi Klein.

But what…so a lot of what they talk about in this book ("The Shock Doctrine") is this thing called: Problem, Reaction, Solution. David Icke talks about this as well…

A lot of people talk about this…this 3-Act…how things get done. So, this Problem, Reaction, Solution. This is a 3-Act Structure.

And so, what you have…you have the Hero's Journey. You have the Problem (Beginning Act), the Reaction (Middle Act), and the Solution (Final Act).

That's one way to look at it. How…how Joseph Campbell like to look at it was…there was…so you've got like…oops (problems with computer) …nope…is it this one?

Anyways. At the beginning. There's a few…the beginning's very important for any story. Because that's how you hook people in to tell them the rest of the story.

And so, the bigger the problem…or the more people that can identify with that problem. The better chance you have of getting their attention for the rest.

It can become a problem though too. When the problem is too generic. Like it might apply to everyone, but it's just not deep or interesting enough.

So, there's a lot of little techniques in the beginning to hook readers in. There's...they have something called a "Save the Cat" moment. Where they usually...

Well, at the very beginning sometimes they'll use a mystery to draw you in. Like even before...so even before the beginning...before the beginning starts sometimes they'll take a piece. A piece from the middle or end and put it up front.

And so, you're like interested. It's a mystery. "Well, how did they end up in that situation?".

So, there's the mystery and then there's a lot of times, like I said, a "Save the Cat" moment where the author or the storyteller tries to get you to identify and sympathize with the character. The Hero.

So, you have the "Save the Cat". And then...so they get you to identify with the Hero. And then usually...about...they try to establish that right away. A mystery and an identification. Within probably the first few minutes. The first 5 minutes.

And then what happens around 10-15 minutes in. They have something called an "Inciting Incident". Which is a shake up to the Hero's normal life.

And so, you identify with this guy. The inciting incident that's the beginnings of a problem. Or that's when the Hero becomes aware that…things are getting a little weird from his normal comfort zone.

So, you get an inciting incident. It kind of disrupts the Hero's life. And so, he's kind of…he's kind of confronting this problem for a little while.

And then, usually what marks the Act break between Act 1 and Act 2 is a "Call to Action".

So, you have the Hero in his normal life. You've got an incident where his normal life gets disrupted. And then he's got a choice.

He's presented with a Call to Action. So, he has to decide what to do with this problem. Is he going to do something about it? What is he going to do with it? How is it going to…

And a lot of times you'll get a refusal from the Hero. Like, "I don't want any part of this".

But a lot of times he'll come back. You know, he'll re-evaluate that…OK, this is a problem that I need to do something about. And so, that becomes the middle.

So, you have the Hero. His normal life is disrupted. He's got a problem. He gets a call to action. So, now he's neck deep in this problem that disrupted his normal life.

And this middle section, a lot of times it's referred to as the "Fun & Games". It might not be fun & games for the Hero. While he's going through it because there's a lot of peril and danger and uncertainty.

So, for him it's an adventure. It's fun & games and he's dealing with the problem. There's evil forces. But for the audience. It's riveting. It's fascinating. Because they want to see how the Hero deals with it.

And so, these fun & games they kind of…like if you had a music track…that will build up in intensity.

So, these problems. You'll get some small problems. And then the problems grow bigger. Like a sine wave. Bigger and bigger and then so…

What usually marks the Act break between Act 2 and Act 3 is...a climax. Or...so the problems have gotten so big that...there's gotta be a resolution to them.

They can't get any bigger. Like there's...just a...there's gotta be a resolution.

So, the Hero. He's confronted with a problem. Tries to...sometimes tries to deny it. Finally takes the call to action. Deals with it. It gets worse and worse and worse. And then...

This is kind of...I guess what it is...what I was talking about with...so, the Hero's going to be changed by this interaction. The fun & games. So, this changes him. How he deals with the problem.

And it's not just an intellectual understanding. Logical, rational understanding. The Hero's also going to come to a different emotional understanding. Or intuitive understanding. That maybe...maybe he knew all along?

So, yeah. That will make for a satisfying drama. Is an emotional understanding. But also, you know, an intellectual understanding.

OK. So, that's kind of how the mechanics of drama work.

Very, very, very simplified.

And so, the reason I bring that stuff up. Is, like I said, it's not just…it's not just Hollywood. You've got this same dramatic structure playing out in…Religions…in Politics…in just our everyday life.

If you can sometimes realize…this stuff is going on…it can…

And it's going to come up again. Like I said, this is something I had brought up over the last couple episodes. And it's something that's going to come up again.

Because I was going to get into…I was going to apply a lot of this stuff to…Marketing. And Propaganda. And, you know, Mysteries. And how…how people get you to listen to their story.
How advertisers get you to listen to their story. How government propaganda gets you to listen. The…

So, it's very…it's going to come up again.

OK. Let me get back to aliens before this…appears to get way off track.

But, before. This is one last thing about emotions and intellectual understanding.

So, this is Seth again. Jane Roberts and Seth. And this stands out to me. Because Seth is…Seth is normally got a…Seth is normally even…his energy is very uplifting…and positive…and constructive.

Usually very measured in his approach. And this is one of the only times he gets a little fire and brimstone.

And what he's…so this is from…. someone had asked me on the internet, "What do I absolutely need to know about consciousness? What's the low down?"

And I think Seth kind of nails it on the head. And he's saying we've taken ego understanding, the reasoning intellect, we've taken it as far as we can go. And what needs to happen is there needs to be an acceptance of the whole.

Of the intuitive knowledge. The emotional. Let me go ahead and read this for the people who are just listening. So, this is from "The Unknown Reality Volume 1" page 113.

I think "The Unknown Reality" …I think it's the 3rd or the 4th…or 5th book. That was published. There's a lot of early sessions of Seth that aren't published.

That I'm actually thinking of putting up a Kickstarter so I can go look through some of the unpublished stuff. I guess all of the unpublished Seth material is sitting in the Yale Library. There's like 500 boxes worth of stuff I think.

The Early Sessions have been published. But there's also a lot of unpublished stuff.

But anyways. This quote from "The Unknown Reality Volume 1" page 113. What Seth says is:

"Man's unconscious knowledge is becoming more and more consciously apparent. Ego consciousness must now be familiarized with its roots, or it will turn into something else.

This will be done under and with the direction of an enlightened and expanding egotistical awareness, that can organize the hereto neglected knowledge -or- it will be done at the expense of the reasoning intellect, leading to a rebirth of superstition, chaos, and the unnecessary war between reason and intuitive knowledge.

When, at this point now, of mankind's development, his emerging unconscious knowledge is denied by his institutions, then it will rise up despite those institutions, and annihilate them. Cult after cult will emerge, each unrestrained by the use of reason, because reason will have denied the existence of rampant unconscious knowledge, disorganized and feeling only its own ancient force."

This doesn't sound good folks.

And it's easy to see why. Because he's saying there's, "rampant unconscious knowledge". It's out there. But the reasoning intellect is just denying it. He uses this word over and over, deny.

So, that relates to the drama we were just talking about. There's an emotional understanding. Intuitive knowledge. It's gotta be recognized.

Alright. So, let's get back to aliens.

Well, OK, before the aliens. This is a real interesting story if…and it relates to…and so now we're getting into the aliens.

This relates to the symbolism I was telling in the last story. With the angel on one eye and the demon on the other.

Howard Stern has a really interesting story to tell about meeting the Devil out in desert of…I think I want to say Arizona.

But it's 28 minutes long. You can find that on YouTube. Howard Stern meets the Devil.

So, if you want you can check that out. And then…so, hang on. I need to…hang on…

OK. One more thing I wanted to point out. About drama and movies. And emotions. Is…this movie is really good. Because it kind of takes that structure and throws it out the sink. Or gets really creative with it.

This is a really good movie ("Memento" by Christopher & Jonathan Nolan). And it's also funny if you talk about synchronicities because in this movie they get into what we were talking about…

I had said Hubbard's son had a suspicious death with diabetes complications. And so, that's one of the plot points of this movie. Is this guy's wife was murdered with Insulin. Diabetes medication.
So, I thought I'd bring that up because it's a good movie.

Anyways. Back to the aliens though.

Yeah, I want to get into some of the symbolism. Of…I lost my campfire. Hang on.

OK. One more thing. Because I was just bringing up movies. There's another movie. That I'm going to talk about later on. After…one of my other telepathic stories.

So, I want to talk about that movie later (the movie "Pi" by Darren Aronofksy).

But for now I want to get more into the symbolism for that first story.

Not just the angels and demons, but all of it. Like I was talking about with the lightning bolt. And the ripping out of the body. And the reptilian stuff.

So, I want to take a little closer look at that symbolism.

And I think the first thing to point out with that stuff. Like I brought up in the last episode…at the time I was taking a lot of that stuff personally. Like emotionally.

I had, at the time, an emotional understanding of it. And like I was just talking about…how there's…the intellectual-reasoning intellect isn't the only way to understand the world.

So, when this stuff…when this story was happening. Yeah, I took a lot of it personally.

It was really the only way I had at the time to analyze it. Was just an emotional understanding.

Because I hadn't read, you know, a lot of books on aliens or UFOs or spirituality or magick or the occult.

I didn't really know anything – intellectually at the time. All I had was emotional understanding.

So, I had mentioned how I thought the…I guess I'll work backwards here a little bit. So, the angels and demons that they put on my eyes. I was very…that kind of upset me (laughing).

Because nobody likes to see themselves as the villain or as bad. You know, I've never really looked at myself as having any bad.

And so, that kind of upset me when they telepathically projected this message that possibly half of me, there was something wrong it.

So, that kind of upset me. And so, I didn't accept that. I got the message and I personally…I didn't believe that. So, I was looking for a more intellectual explanation for that.

Kind of how I mentioned with the shapeshifting into the reptile or the serpent or the snake. I had brought up the possibility that…they had taken a look. Or they had gotten some information with the beam. And then they were giving me stuff.

Maybe they had looked into my future and seen how I was going to start this Fire Snake Project. And so, they were kind of showing me my future a little bit.

So, I'm wondering with the Angels and Demons. You know, I'm sure they could have projected that symbolism into my mind. I think it's interesting that it was projected onto eyes.

With my eyes being one of the significant events in my life. The healing of them. So, where they put the symbol I think is important or significant. They put them onto my eyes and...

What that symbol is implying is...two separate...is a separateness. You know, a good and a bad or evil.

So, if you don't take that personally they could be talking about the Universe as a whole or humanity as a whole. How there's good and bad parts to it.

Or it could even be...a reference to how our consciousness seems to be getting ready to "split". Or produce some kind of offspring. A new type of consciousness.

So, maybe they were referring to that. Because a lot of times parents will have a child and they'll wonder...you know (giggles)...they'll see a lot of...they'll look at that as a demon or see a lot of bad things.

Not just a physical…actual child. But people talk about their inventions as children. Or authors talk about their books as children. Their creative products a lot of artists look at those as children.

And a lot of times those children can take on a life of their own that the creator never intended.

So, I guess that's one of the interesting ways to look at it.

Another interesting way with the angels and demons. You also have…there's even a book by, Dan Brown. The author of "The Da Vinci Code".

He's got a book called "Angels and Demons". So, it's also possible that the symbolism could have been referring to…I guess if you look at it in Religious…as far as Religion.

So, we've had…we've kind of had one…a couple big religions for the past few thousand years. And so, maybe that could be an allusion to…a new religion springing up.

An old religion falling and a new religion gaining momentum. So, obviously that old religion is going to look at that new religion as, you know, demonic.

You could look at it from that angle. Actually, I think the plot line of this book ("Angels & Demons" by Dan Brown) is pretty interesting.

Because you have...where's the summary of this? So, one of the plot lines is...you have...here it is: "Langdon's worst fears...when a messenger of the illuminati says they have hidden an unstoppable time bomb at the very heart of Vatican City"

Now, this will probably get too close to conspiracy...for some. But this symbolism: unstoppable time bomb at the very heart of Vatican City.

You know...I think it's interesting...what happens a lot of times. I think what happens a lot of authors, creative people, tune into stuff.

And they might put stuff in their work that ends up being prophetic in nature.

Because in the "Conversations with Nostradamus" that I keep bringing up. One of the stories…or one of the quatrains…well, a lot of the quatrains deal with what he talks about with the Anti-Christ and the WW3 but…

The details of that is that he…and he talks about the downfall of the Catholic Church and how there's only going to be a couple more Popes.

But how he describes the downfall of the Catholic Church playing out…is through…is through espionage.

He's saying the Anti-Christ is going to actually have an agent inside the Vatican. And I think he might even say that this agent will eventually become Pope.

So, if you look at that agent of the Anti-Christ infiltrating the Vatican…that's kind of an "unstoppable time bomb". So, you've got that symbolism. And then you've got…

Well, that's an interesting concept…authors using magic. I'll get back to that. I think…if you're looking along those lines. Jack London in "The Star Rover".

He talks about. That whole book is about Astral Projection.

The hero of that story is in prison. They put him in a strait jacket. And he learns how to astral project out of the strait jacket. And so that whole book is stories of him astral projecting to past lives. Past reincarnational lives.

It's interesting there's a lot of…you gotta wonder how a lot of these authors come up with some of the details they do in some of their books.

One of the other…Ken Follett "Pillars of the Earth". This is another good one. Where I have…I'm wondering if he gets a lot of the details…12th century tale…building of a mighty Gothic cathedral.

You know…where did he get…how did he get such details of the 12th century? Was he tuning into, either intentionally or unconsciously, into a past life that he had lived?

And then in pop culture you also have. One of the funny things going around the internet. Yeah, you got…is this it? Yeah, "The Simpsons" had a…if you look at this image (Donald Trump as President in the year 2000) …there's some…

So, I think that stuff happens a lot more than people know about. Because I don't think their looking for it.

That's some of the angels and demons' symbolism.

Those are some interesting angles I think to look at that.

Then I guess...moving backwards. The lightning bolt.

Like I said. I initially thought that could have been a warning. They were angry.

Maybe, I had thought...well, I thought at first they were angry they couldn't tear my soul out. So, they hit me with the lightning bolt.

And then I was also thinking...not only were they angry, but it was a warning for the future, "Don't talk about this".

These were like emotional understandings. Or emotional reactions.

But it could have been...the heart symbolism. You know, it went through my heart. That's where it felt like the epicenter was.

Were they getting at something like…humanity's got some…heartbreaking …events. We're going to have to deal with? That are really going to stagger us as a species? You know, maybe set us back? Or really get us to re-evaluate?

That could also be a future symbol, like I said. It could also…like I said, I had an emotional understanding at the time, but it could also be a future thing to take into mind.

And then moving backwards again.

There was the soul ripping out. And, at the time, personally…there was…I wasn't sure what to make of that.

It was…obviously, it was unpleasant. So, one of the things I'm wondering is…well, anytime you move…anytime you start to look at something differently or the paradigm shifts. You move into a paradigm shift.

Where you look at things differently. That can be uncomfortable. Because you're letting go of things that were more familiar. And so, there's a little bit of pain involved with a move to a different viewpoint. Or a different outlook.

And the symbolism there too. They were really concentrating on the soul. They were ripping that out.

So, if we are moving to a different paradigm, that might be a little painful, what is that paradigm going to entail?

Is it going to…is that new paradigm going to include more recognition of the spirit?

Because that was what was happening in my little encounter. I was getting my soul ripped out it felt like. So, that was something I was having to pay attention to.

Maybe that's what this new paradigm is going to bring?

Like I was talking about with the Seth quote. This rampant unconscious knowledge. This spiritual knowledge is going to be something we're just going to have to…figure out…the significance of it.

And moving back again in that story to the reptilian symbols…

That could also apply to this primitive, unconscious knowledge. Those aspects of ourselves.

You know people talk about reptilian as the primitive part of ourselves, or the primitive brain. So, maybe that's some more symbolism of the future…of what we're going to encounter…or have to contend with?

This primitive, unconscious, spiritual…issues…or realities.

There's a bunch more I want to say about that stuff. But I think I'm going to go ahead and move into the other stories, and then call back to that stuff when it comes up.

So, the second story of that month. OK, give me one second.

OK, so I want to get into telling the strictly telepathic story that happened a couple weeks later. After the big dramatic story that I've been telling and analyzing a little bit.

Before I get into the telepathic story though. I do want to bring up a few things about telepathy. Like I did in the first couple parts of this series.

You know, I had brought up…I had brought up examples of other stories of people who had reported classical, characteristic, textbook alien stuff like beams into the head. Or shutting down of willpower. Or missing time. Or screen memories.

Those are reported a lot with aliens. But telepathy is another one of the big things that gets reported alongside aliens, a lot.

I did say that I had some messages that I don't know where they came from. And those are different than the alien telepathy. I'm separating them right now at least.

Like I said, that whole month I was getting…it was just weird stuff and I haven't fully sorted it out yet.

Some of the…like one of the messages was just like a booming voice out of the Heavens or something. It was just like…and it was real…it sounded like almost Biblical, like…"40 years of 40 days of…"

You know, something like that. And the reason why I'm separating that from the alien…I'm calling it the alien telepathy is because the alien telepathy it did have a lot of the features that people describe in telepathy with aliens.

Like a very…almost robotic like voice. Almost machine like. I don't want to say metallic, but almost…distant. Very cool. There was some emotion there, but almost computer like. Just…

Not like this weird message…this booming voice from the Heavens about, "40 days of 40 years…of".

That though I think is interesting. That message. Because a lot times you will get…you will get weird stuff with aliens…what I'm thinking with that 40…I'm thinking I'm coming up on my 40th birthday. Here in a few months.

And it's interesting that a lot of these stories happened a few years or several years back. Again, I'm wondering if somehow they were seeing into the future.

Or even controlling the future. Because people talk about…Dolores Cannon touches on this in some of her alien books, like "The Custodians", or "Keepers of the Garden".

She talks about…because she recorded all her hypnosis sessions with audio. And when she was working with the alien stuff. She said she was having problems with sometimes…with her tape recordings…sometimes tapes would disappear.

For like years or something. And then they would show back up. And she was thinking that they were kind of rationing out. Or controlling when some of this information was going to be available to the public.

So, yeah, that's what I'm wondering with my experiences is that…whoever it was kind of knew…I wouldn't be able to talk about this stuff for a few years yet?

I think Uri Geller had similar problems to Dolores Cannon. With tapes…with tape recording of stuff…getting erased. Or getting misplaced or showing back up again.

That was when he was doing a lot of work or research with Andrija…I'm not even going to try to say his last name (giggle - Andrija Puharich). Let me see (browsing computer) …no, not that. Hmm. Probably remote viewing…yeah. Yeah, this book ("Uri: A journal of the mystery of Uri Geller" by Andrija Puharich).

But anyways…they were having similar problems where things would disappear and come back.

As far as the telepathy though, like I said, that's something that gets reported with aliens pretty regularly.

You've got…with the Men in Black phenomenon. That's one of the big things that gets reported is telepathic powers. It says (website - www.ufoevidence.org/documents/doc1707.htm):

"The most disturbing aspect was that the MIB appeared to know intimate family details without there being any logical explanation of how they had come by this knowledge!"

So, Men in Black are using telepathy.

And this is not necessarily aliens, but Edgar Mitchell did experiments with telepathy from the Moon. So, when Apollo 14…he did…so, he was on the Moon.

And he was trying to telepathically communicate back to earth. And they got some pretty good results from that…

He, yeah…he had some stories about Uri Geller. Yeah, this is some interesting stuff. So, Dr. Mitchell…you can look at his telepathy experiments.

Yeah, Dr. Puharich. He was also doing…he did a lot of telepathy experiments with mushrooms. You can read about some of those in…I think it's "The Sacred Mushroom". Yeah, this one (referring to website).

Another good book that gets into telepathy is this one, "Psychic Warfare: Threat or Illusion?"

So, this book talks a lot about the Russian experiments with telepathy. Well, it talks about…it gives a nice overview of all the countries. The United States, Russia. This book also talks about those Edgar Mitchell experiments. So, this isn't necessarily aliens, but it's talking about telepathy. All these people.

But telepathy is associated with aliens a lot.

And, yeah. Going back most recently. You've got…this is Dr. Steven Greer who I brought up in the last episode. Who is working with the idea that some of these alien abductions might be false flag. Staged by the government.

But, as far as Dr. Greer and aliens and telepathy. What he does…currently. Is he does contact expeditions. So, this is CE-5.

Close Encounters. Close encounters of the 5th kind. You guys might be familiar with the movie, "Close Encounters of the 3rd Kind". 5th Kind just means that you're the one who goes looking for it.

You're not waiting for the ETs to come to you. You're going out on expeditions trying to contact them.

I haven't been on an expedition personally. But one of the major…from what I understand one of the major…tools. They use to get a manifestation from the UFOs or the aliens is telepathy.

Broadcasting intentions of a group of people. "Thought – specifically consciousness – is the primary mode of initiating contact."

And so, Dr. Steven Greer is using telepathy as a tool. That's going on right now.

A little while back you had a very interesting individual, Ted Owens. Who claimed to be in contact with Space People. And Ted Owens also wrote a couple books telling people how they could contact them on their own.

He was using the same technique that Dr. Greer is using in the CE-5 initiative…is to…is telepathy. He claimed he was in telepathic contact.

Yeah, this is a good book. This one ("The PK Man: A True Story of Mind Over Matter" by Jeffrey Mishlove, Ph.D.). That's all about Ted Owens.

And he's interesting, not just his alien encounters. But he…so, PK that's psychokinesis. Which I am going to address in a…future episode.

But, he also thought he was the reincarnation of Moses. So, with this one person, Ted Owens, you've got aliens and telepathic communication. You've got psychokinesis. And then you've also got the religious angle with Moses.

So, that's a really interesting story. So, that was about 50 years ago.

Currently, you have Dr. Greer and the CE-5. 50 years ago you had Ted Owens. He was also taking people out on expeditions to contact aliens.

And then, if you go back even further...so, this is where history moves in spirals. So, you had Dr. Greer, Ted Owens, and then Aleister Crowley...I guess 50 years before Ted Owens.

Early 2oth century, he (Aleister Crowley) was contacting aliens. Lam was the name of the alien that Crowley talked with...telepathically.

And there's a lot of stories or theories or explanations that have popped up around Aleister Crowley and the aliens. About how...you know, The Babylon Working, and they think a Portal was enlarged because you had Hubbard and Parsons...

Like I said I might get into that whole thing in another episode.

But, yeah. One of the…so, OK. (Laughing) I think I'm going to…I think I'm going to…I think I'm going to be a little bit reckless. Because (laughing intensifies) how I…because there's…also telepathy involved with Bigfoot (more laughing).

Yeah, people, you know. So, people are probably thinking I'm being reckless because a lot of people won't even accept aliens.

So, if you start talking about Bigfoot…there's…it's…now that's like "double secret recklessness".

But, this is an interesting…this is Bigfoot Field Researchers Organization.

And this talks about a telepathic encounter in…1976 in Pennsylvania. You really…you should read this story. It's really interesting.

But, basically. This guy. He was with his friend, skipping school. And they went to go…they went to go hunt some squirrels with a crossbow or something like that. And…telepathically. Yeah.

He says…he describes the Bigfoot. But then it telepathically talked to him and it said, "If you hurt me I'm going to kill you both". Him and his friend.

I think this is important though about what he was eating. He said something about…hmm…chewing a piece of tree. Chewing it like it was…how you see cows chewing cud.

But, this is not the only time with Bigfoot and telepathy. Actually, Seth…Seth, talks about Bigfoot.

He doesn't say telepathy specifically. Here's what he says about Bigfoot. This is Seth. This is I think one of the later books. It might even be one of the last books. This is "The Way Towards Health", page 22-24.

And so Jane had actually been…she had seen a TV show or she had been reading about Bigfoot. So, when Seth came through he started…the reason he started talking about Bigfoot is because she was interested in it. And so what he says is:

"There are many, many species that man has not discovered, in all the categories of life – insects onward.

There are multitudinous species of viruses and so forth that man has not encountered and recognized".

– I'm going to have to come back to this statement for sure. Because Seth does talk about viruses a lot. And he even says there's some invisible viruses. We're not quite aware of yet. And they might even have something to do with our evolution and our DNA.

But, he's saying there's viruses we haven't recognized. Has not encountered and recognized.

"…and there are connections between viruses and other species of living matter that remain unknown. There are indeed two different kinds of upward-walking mammals, much like your own species, but much larger, and with infinitely keener senses."

That sounds like better psychic powers. Telepathy. He doesn't specifically say telepathy. But, infinitely keener senses sure sounds like telepathy.

So, they're much larger. Amazingly swift. Through scent alone they're aware of the presence of man at least several miles away.

Vegetable matter is their main diet. I was just talking about with this guy (1976 Pennsylvania Bigfoot sighting) …said he was chewing on a piece of tree.

And so here's…there is a discrepancy though.

Because Seth is saying these creatures can tell when a man is around the area. Just from their scent. He's saying, "through scent alone". Even though they have these other infinitely keener senses.

But in this story (Pennsylvania 1976)…I think this guy says that…the property he had his Bigfoot encounter on…it's in the middle of Levittown. The property…about a mile square each way.

So, it makes you wonder. Why this Bigfoot…how they were able to get so close? And…could this encounter have been…have been staged like I mentioned earlier how aliens can kind of hold back material like I said with the 40 years' stuff? Maybe…who knows?

That's…so, you've got telepathy with Bigfoots. And I think…I'm not sure…well, I did want to go back to…

I did mention how Saturday Night Live had made fun of the anal probing…situation. In the "Communion" story. So, Saturday Night Live had kind of turned that anal probing into a pop culture meme or joke.

And if you remember back…Saturday Night Live…with Dan Akroyd. They did a lot of skits with aliens. If you remember the Coneheads…where (giggling) they drink beer and eat potato chips.

But, Dan Akroyd, he had an encounter with Men in Black. And I don't know which show he talks about it in (or YouTube video) …

He's got a bunch of great stories. Especially from growing up. I think his…grandfather…his family. They used to hold séances. Trying to contact spirits and stuff.

But, I think his Men in Black encounter. That came about because he was wanting to do a TV series. Dealing with paranormal, UFO stuff like that.

And I think when he was making that TV series he had…a Men in Black encounter with…some type of dark Cadillac. That just…he saw it…and it turned the corner and just disappeared or something.

I don't think there was any telepathy there…but, I wanted to bring that stuff up because I mentioned with the Saturday Night Live connection. And obviously he has the Crystal Skull Vodka…which the Crystal Skulls are a real interesting thing to look into…

So, my story about the aliens and telepathy though.

Hang on. Let me get something to drink.

OK. Actually, there's a few more things I wanted to run through really quick here. Actually, these 3 things (pointing to computer screen).

So, I think a lot of people know this. But, Tesla…Tesla claimed he was getting messages from Space. I don't remember the details exactly. But, you can…there's a ton of stuff written about…that he thought…they might've been…Mars.

But, he was receiving them through his electronics. I don't think they came mentally. I think he thought there was a message in what his electronic equipment was picking up.

I think he also had a pretty…a pretty…a mystical side too. Like Einstein did.

So, you can read into that.

And then talking about Scientific people. Scientists who have had interesting encounters. So, Tesla was thinking from Outer Space.

Descartes, who I guess a lot of people consider like the founder of Modern Science. So, in…I'm not sure what year it was…but, anyways, Descartes had a dream. And in his dream an angel appeared to him and said, "The conquest of nature is to be achieved through measure and number".

And that revelation lay the basis for modern science. So, that's interesting that modern science is based on a dream. A dream with an angel. Like we brought up "Altered States". And an angel.

You know, a lot of scientists have had visions come to them like that. I think the scientist who found the structure of the benzene ring. Yeah, that was a dream too:

"He said that after he had discovered the ring shape of the benzene molecule after having a reverie or day-dream of a snake seizing its own tail. This is an ancient symbol known as the ouroboros".

I think these are some stories people already know about. Maybe they don't. So, I'm just bringing them up because I think there pretty interesting.

So, that's the snake eating its own tail. The ouroboros.

Yeah, you had Descartes, Tesla…and even Joseph Smith who founded the Mormon Religion. That was also an angel. An angel came to him and…

I'm not sure exactly how the story goes. Here it is:

"One night he was visited by an angel named Moroni, who revealed the location of a buried book…"

So, but this story I think is interesting because you know who else talks about that Joseph Smith story? One of my favorite books, the "Conversations with Nostradamus" by Dolores Cannon.

This is Volume 1. Of that trilogy. I'm not sure the chapter. OK, the Great Genius. So, this is quatrain VII-14. And, so he says:

"A minor event this quatrain refers to is an event that has already taken place. In the early 19th century there was a man who came into possession of some Egyptian documents of ancient times that were discovered in some tombs. And this man had a trace of psychic ability. Through this he gave an interpretation of these documents that was partially correct and partially incorrect.

So, here: "History moves in spirals". I said that earlier in the episode. But, he says…" came into possession of some Egyptian documents of ancient times…". I don't know how he got them…

Yeah, so. This episode is getting a little long. So, my story…

Or the telepathic incident.

What happened with that was. So, that strange month was going on…and it was…I'm pretty sure it was Sunday morning because I was watching some golf on TV.

So, it was probably either Saturday or Sunday morning because they don't usually televise golf on Thursday and Friday mornings. So, I was watching TV and messing around on the computer and…

I just…I don't…I think I might have been
doing…yeah, I was doing some… I don't know what
to call it.

(Chuckling) I think it was mixture between automatic
writing and tarot or divination. Anyways, so this
voice came through in my head. And like I said, it
sounded very robotic almost. Very…like a
metallic/machiney.

And so what it said was…I think the first thing it said
was, "sexy time". (Giggling) Like, Borat has that
saying, "sexy time"?

So, I was a little confused by that. The way it…the
way he was speaking at the time, I almost thought it
was a question. Like I mentioned how a lot of people
when they encounter aliens, the aliens ask them,
"What time is it?" So, I thought he was asking me
about "sexy time".

Like, I thought he wanted me to explain human sexy
time (laughter). Like, when people they get asked,
"What time is it?" They usually give an answer to the
alien. Like 2:30 or whatever. (More laughter) Like that
time would make any sense to the alien. Like, my
explanation of sexy time would make any sense.

So, I wasn't quite sure…he said, "sexy time". And then he said, "doggy style". So, that's when I was kind of like…now, I'm really confused (more laughing).

Does he…he wants to know specifically about…doggy style sexy time? And why we do it in that position?

So, I was…(giggling)…I actually did try to explain.

And I think I did use as an explanation…I don't even know if it's right. Because I've been re-evaluating a lot of stuff recently.

But, this was a book I had read…I think back in college. I think called, "The Naked Ape?" Yeah, this book…one of the ideas in this book…the controversial classic (reading the cover of the book).

So, I don't know if these ideas are accepted. But I think one of the ideas was…as far as our evolution. So, if we went from hunched over on all fours to walking…to upright. I think in apes…one of the theories is that their behind, or their rear end, is like a visual signal. For like sex.

And I think one of this guy's theories was that…so, when man went 4 legs up to 2 legs…he also needed a visual signal, a sexual signal on his chest.

Like, he had his behind from the rear. Where you could see that sexual signal. So, then when he went from 4 to 2 legs he needed another visual signal on his chest. And that's the reason women developed breasts.

Because this author (Desmond Morris) was comparing…Well, why do apes not have very large breasts? And I think he said, basically, that we grew a rear end on our chest.

I don't know if I agree with that. I'd have to go back and re-evaluate with the knowledge I have now. Like I said, I read that in college. And I believed a lot of things differently back then.

But that was the only explanation I had for what I thought was a weird question. From the alien.

So, I proceeded to tell him about that book (laughing). And now, it's almost kind of embarrassing…when I think about it. If I think about…I'm going to give that dude anything he doesn't already know.

So, I'm thinking it wasn't a question. He's not asking me anything. But I go ahead and proceed to arrogantly (chuckling)…give him answers to stuff.

And now…well, OK. Now, what I'm thinking is that he was telling me something.

He was giving me a message. And I think he was being funny about it. I think he was telling me I was being messed with.

Like, I was being "fucked with". Right? Like, sexy time? People are fucking with you. Right? Like, "sexy time" …" doggy style". People are fucking with you.

Well, that's what I'm thinking now. I could be wrong. And in another couple years…maybe there's another deeper meaning to that.

I'm sure…the symbolism of sex. That's like our number 1, or one of…yeah, a lot of these symbols…and I think that's going to be interesting to see how I'm thinking about this stuff in a couple years.

So, after I gave him that answer. The next thing he said…he was probably getting inpatient (giggle).

Because he did seem a little frustrated or angry…that I didn't…so, the next thing he said was…

"Only prime numbers". And so…after I had given this long response about (chuckle) human sexual behavior. He said, "Only prime numbers".

And I…had no clue what to make of that either. Like with the confusing, "sexy time", "doggy style" …and so…(sighs)…I guess…well, "Only prime numbers".

Maybe I should just start typing numbers? And… (more sighs) …and he'll tell me when to stop on the right number like an Ouija board? I had no idea.

So, I started typing numbers. And yeah. He got angry at that (lots of laughing).

Not angry. But, inpatient. Like, this guy has no clue what I'm trying to tell him.

But, OK. With the symbolism of that. OK. Now, that I've thought about that some more. I'm thinking…I'm thinking that might be another message.

About…I think…so, "Only prime numbers". And one of the things about nature is that…there's no…there's no 2 things that are identical. Everything is unique. Like, you have snowflakes.

They say…no 2 snowflakes are alike. Everything in nature is unique and different. And it is interesting that…yeah, I think there's some…deep symbolism there.

And, you know, I'm just trying to understand that. Just starting to try to understand…who knows? I could be way off track like I was a couple years ago.

So, that's what he said. So, that was that story.

OK. Yeah, there is…that's what I brought up earlier…why I brought up that movie, "Pi". And one of the interesting things they talk about in this movie…this is a really good movie by the way 1998…

So, this was a movie about: A paranoid mathematician searches for a key number that will unlock the universal patterns found in nature.

And...one of the memorable quotes...here it is...no...yeah. So, Maximillian Cohen [to Rabbi Cohen and a group of Kabbalists]...he's been searching for...what did I say? He's a paranoid mathematician searches for a key number that will unlock the universal patterns found in nature.

After, so this is towards the end of the movie. I don't think this is spoiling anything, but...so...he says to the Rabbi and the group of Kabbalists:

"It's just a number. I'm sure you've written down every 216-digit number. You've translated all of them. You've intoned them all. Haven't you? What's it gotten you? The number is nothing! It's the meaning. It's the syntax. It's what's between the numbers. You haven't understood it. It's because it's not for you! I've got it. I've got it! And I understand it and I'm going to see it. Rabbi, I was chosen!"

So, maybe that's what the alien was getting at with the, "Only prime numbers"? It's not...you know...it's the unique...space?

But, what's also interesting when you take that statement into account. So, this movie was 1998. One of the other...interesting movies that came out around the same time 1999. And you're talking about numbers.

And looking between the numbers. That's what all these (referring to the movie "The Matrix" and the cascading numbers from the opening credit sequence) ...are.

And there was a lot of...1999 was a good year for movies. I think Fight Club came out in 1999 too. It was a really good year. And if you want to look into the mind...that's a...good...place.

So, yeah. That was the telepathic story.

And then I had said that there was an orb story. So, the story with the orb.

This was no longer March. This was about a year or two later? But since that month of March there's still been strange stuff going on. It hasn't...

It's kind of relented from getting...from big dramatic shapeshifting events. But, there's still a lot of strange stuff going on.

But, obviously this has gotten really long already (the videocast). I can't…I will address a lot of it. Down the road. But, the orb…so, about a year or two later. For some reason I got up. I went to bed and got up around 2 or 3 in the AM. Because I couldn't sleep. And I don't know why.

And this happens a lot with alien stories. People get…feel like they get summoned somewhere. They were sitting in their house and they feel an urge to go outside. Or go look in the woods. Or go do something. And a lot of times they say they don't know why they were doing that.

And that's not something I do a lot. Is go for walks in the middle of the night. But, it's interesting too…3 O'clock. Around 3 O'clock is around when this happened. It might have been a little earlier. It might have been around 2. But 3 O'clock they call that the "witching hour".

So, yeah. For some reason I got disturbed out of my sleep. And I kind of knew…that I wasn't going…I don't know…I knew I wasn't going to get back to sleep.

I don't think I quite did it for exercise. I think…I don't know… I just…a walk sounded like a good idea. And when I say it that way…it almost sounds like. It might've been a very primitive attempt at…pushing a thought into someone's head.

"I think a walk would be a good idea". Who knows though? That might've been my thought.

But, so I went for a walk and I got near the beginning of my neighborhood. And it doesn't make sense to be looking over your shoulder. Not at that time of night. Because no one's out.
For some reason I looked over my shoulder and…I would probably say…across the street, but in the backyard of the across the street.

So, I don't know how many feet wide the typical street and lots are in my neighborhood. I'm guessing…I'm bad with yardage and stuff like that…or feet.

It would be very easy to go measure it right now. So, I don't want to give an estimate that's way off. But, you know, it wasn't more than a couple hundred…I'm thinking of kicking a field goal…so, 50 yards or less.

Maybe closer. But, yeah it was…it kind of had to be…a little bit away. Because at first I thought I might have been the Moon.

Because it was about the size of a basketball. Up in the…not much farther above the houses. That's why it was so strange. I'm like, "That's a strange place for the Moon to be (giggle). That low in the sky"

But, then it went like…directly down. Fast. So, it was like a whitish orb. Glowing like the moon would. About the size of a…I want to say basketball. But, it's hard to estimate size if it was 40, 50 yards away.

Well, that's how I kind of rationalized it at the time. There was this glowing thing that went directly down. So, in my mind the first thing…I didn't think…UFO.

In my mind, my first thought was, "Well, that's strange that my neighbor would be throwing glowing basketballs in the air…straight up in the air and catching them on the way back down. At 3 O'clock in the morning."

(Chuckling) It's entirely possible that's what he was doing. You know, I can't say for sure. All I know is it's not something I've ever seen before.

But, I didn't have any other strange effects from it. No, burning my skin or my eyes. Or, no telepathy or no noises.

The only thing strange, like I said, I don't normally go for a walk at that time of night.

So, who knows? But, like I said, also with strange things how they attract each other. So, maybe that's kind of what's been going on.

The strange things just keep attracting strange things. And this thing…maybe he saw like…what are all these other strange things going on? Who knows?

Anyways. Someone else who talks about that a lot is John Keel, I think. He's the one who investigated The Mothman. And a lot of the stranger phenomenon.

But, he reported a lot of strange stuff started happening to him. When he started looking into that stuff. He started having problems with his phone. And Men in Black type people.

So, I haven't gotten any of that stuff. Like I said, it has been building up.

There's only so much I can fit into each of these episodes. This is really long already so…

I think I covered most of the stuff. I wanted to. In the outline at the beginning. I finished talking about a lot of the symbolism with the other stories. Random stuff popped up like it always does.

I got to tell a couple new stories. Not till the very end. Sorry, about that if that was the only thing you came for. And I think we just got a little bit into the symbolism with…prime numbers and…human reproduction.

But there's also…yeah, you can get into the circular orb energy. And I am going to…I did get a little bit into the crop circles. You got more circular…I talked about that in those…blog posts. That'll probably be…oops…the next trilogy I said.

But, I need a little break from aliens. It's just been…a lot of them. So…we'll get into that then.

So, alright. I think that's it. Thanks for…thanks for tuning in.

END

CHAPTER 1 – STEALING FIRE

"A man contains all that is needed to make up a tree; likewise, a tree contains all that is needed to make up a man. Thus, finally, all things meet in all things, but we need a Prometheus to distill it"

- Cyrano de Bergerac, in *The Other World* (1657)

Bandit. This was one of the nicknames friends took to calling me growing up. Nothing major (I can admit to). Pens, lighters, cigarettes, beer. The usual teenage games. It helped being able to coast on my reputation of being a straight-A "goody two-shoes". Don't get me wrong - that's never who I was. It's just the image teachers and parents had of me. Someone else would always end up taking the blame, and I could almost get away with murder.

Everybody probably knew a guy like this. The Eddie Haskell type. But without the overdone super-polite manners in my case. Just the nice, quiet, sweet boy. So, there must be something to what they say about the quiet ones. This talent would come in handy later in life when playing poker for a living after graduating med school.

I'm getting way ahead of myself though. The stolen items weren't even things I really wanted. I had no idea what to do with them once I had them (excluding the beer and cigarettes). I guess it was the thrill. Or the challenge. Or maybe it was playing with the images people had of me in their minds. Either way, I seemed to be good at it - getting away with murder.

And that's a perfect analogy for what happened to me almost a year ago today. In the warm spring air, during college basketball's March madness tournament, when everyone in the nation was feverishly checking to see how badly their brackets had been busted, I was back to my old ways and looking to pull a fast one. It was only information I was after. However, I didn't anticipate the stakes would be life and death. That night I pushed the laws of the natural world a little too far and triggered a near-death-experience (NDE).

NDEs are not as rare as people might think. Polls show 5% of the population have had a NDE. 13 million people just in the United States alone. 774 new cases occurring every day. With another 30 million Americans, or 12% of adults, reporting some type of out-of-the-body experience in their lifetime.

My NDE was different though. Very different.

This was something I deliberately set out to do. An experience that was intentionally courted. And well, I guess that's why we have all those great sayings. Because they were right once again when they admonish - Be careful what you wish for.

The goal had not been to induce my own death. It wasn't an attempt to channel Kiefer Sutherland from the movie Flatliners. If I had known beforehand how it was all going to unfold, you can bet your ass I would have had a team of doctors standing by with all sorts of technology, hooked up to monitors and machines and any drugs needed to jumpstart a resuscitation effort. I just wanted answers. It happens the afterlife was the place they were hiding though.

You can go ahead and pile on here with the jokes or witticisms about curiosity killing the cat or something about nine lives, but the bottom line is - I did get answers. Not in any form that made sense at the time. And not without wracking my brain for a year, trying to remember everything I've ever learned and trying to learn everything I didn't already know. But, without a doubt answers. A whole treasure chests worth. Plunder worthy of a pirate with a nickname like Steel beard or something equally as awesome.

My NDE was also highly unusual for a number of other reasons.

The first being – my thoughts and visualizations are what initiated the cause of death. The human mind really is that powerful. We'll get into that discussion though in the next two chapters and throughout the rest of the book.

Another very strange aspect of my NDE was the way in which I reentered my body. The crossover back to the world of the living actually happened through someone else's body initially, and for a while on my return, I was occupying two bodies simultaneously. We'll do a review and analysis of NDEs in the next chapter, but for now I just want to get the story across without interruption.

So in a way you could say I did get away with murder – my own. And I was very lucky to be "resurrected" through the generous, but not consensual use of another person's body as a link back to the physical world. Another way of putting it is, I was trespassing in God's territory. I had no right to be there. It wasn't my time to visit that realm. But boy there I was, and man was it terrific. Yet on my return, I found myself in a similar situation as my younger days. I had all this stolen property and no idea what to do with it.

Thankfully, a little bit of wisdom does come with age. So instead of chucking things in the trash as I would have before, I set out to understand the deeper meaning behind why other people's things always seemed to accumulate around me. Whether meaningless material objects as a youth, or now higher knowledge that didn't seem to belong to me, a disturbing pattern was revealing itself. The common thread between it all appearing to be mischief.

There had to be a reason for it all. Was it my destiny to be a modern day Prometheus, the Titan from Greek mythology with the wily intelligence, who stole fire from the Gods and gave it to mankind?

Could my penchant for collecting odds and ends or bluffing at the poker table have been some sort of unconscious training program? The introductory level classes on the way to becoming a full blown cat burglar of hidden knowledge? A way to hone one's nerves in preparation for the heist of the millennium in a raid against the Gods?

If that's the case what will my punishment be? (Other than the dirty looks and bad thoughts people are sending my way after reading of my unsavory activities) Will I too, like Prometheus, be chained to a rock, and an eagle sent to eat my regenerating liver day after day for the rest of eternity?

Or worse still, forced into some kind of useful role of serving humanity with these ill-gotten revelations? No longer the master illusionist who controls the show and saws the woman in half to reveal two parts, but reduced to nothing more than a tool, the saw itself, used by higher powers, kept in the dark, and tossed aside when my blades begin to dull?

There I go getting ahead of myself again though (and a little overdramatic). So let's backtrack to the night of my NDE when this all starting getting a little too serious, and see if I can organize my thoughts for you from there.

The Heat is On

We're going to need to return to the scene of the crime. They say not to do this, but criminals like to admire their work. Or so I've heard. I wouldn't know. Like someone famous once said, "I am not a crook". Here we are though, and we're going to have do a re-enactment in order to get anywhere with this. So the obvious burning question everyone is probably dying to ask is - How does one get to a mental state where killing themselves with their thoughts doesn't seem like such a bad idea?

Well, let me tell you. It's not easy. Not easy at all. A good start would be to take a lifetime of crushing disappointment with your fellow human beings. Combine that with equal parts desperate search for answers as to why you feel you're doing everything right, yet everything seems to turn out horribly wrong. Stir it all together, maybe shake once or twice, and there you have it. A perfect murder martini, Mr. Bond. That'll be $17 dollars please.

And I'm going to firmly recommended no one reading at home attempt to duplicate what I'm going to describe here shortly.

I cannot guarantee your safety should you choose to ignore my advice. As mentioned already, I consider myself extremely lucky other human bodies were in the vicinity to provide a gateway back to whatever word you want to describe for whatever plane of existence we're on now is. There is a very good chance if you are successful with my method you may not return, or worse - your body may continue in a coma like state and require hospitalization and expensive medical bills until it eventually expires.

However, I do feel comfortable relaying this story because I know first-hand the amount of courage it takes to do what I did. Trust me, it's no small amount (and you can trust me, I am a doctor. I also stayed at a Holiday Inn Express once too, so you can trust me double. Heck, I'm half Irish as well so let's make it a trifecta of trustworthiness).

Out of total honesty and in no way meant as a brag, one of the top few words I would use to describe myself is fearless. But even I had to back out at the last second on my first attempt with this method. I needed to regroup and fully and absolutely commit to giving up everything I knew in this world.

I don't have much personal experience with real life suicide outside of the few patients I interacted with on my psychiatry rotations in med school.

From what I've heard though, the vast majority who attempt suicide and end up surviving almost always say something very similar. That the last thought after the point of no return was something along the lines of, "I've made a huge mistake". Dismiss these warnings at your own risk.

Back on track again. Here we are at the crime scene. What exactly happened? What circumstances lead to such a heinous act being committed? You said "crushing disappointment" and "desperate searches", but those are just generalities. Why are you so disappointed and desperate? You're a doctor. How bad can your life be? Surely, you drive an S-Class Mercedes and live in a gated community with a Barbie doll wife? Did you have to cut back from three ski trips a year to just one? Is that what this is all about?

We'll review reincarnation in the section on consciousness, but for now I'll just say - since I was a small child, I always remember feeling an overwhelming sense of disappointment. There's no specific reason why I should've felt this way either. Especially if you consider the situation I grew up in. We had money for things. Both my parents were around. My older sister would beat me up like all siblings do, but she was not some sociopathic demon who tortured me mercilessly. Teachers always considered me a favorite. I had good friends through sports.

The only way it makes sense is if a design or complexity exists on a deeper level than we're normally aware of. I am not saying reincarnation happens and this is proof because look at my childhood. The point I'm trying to get across is, logic fails to properly explain it. The tools and knowledge we have right now are inadequate. Our current answers don't really answer a whole lot. And not many seem to notice this or want to find answers. They pretend they know, instead of saying, "Well, we/I don't know". They love to pretend they know.

So my life took some turns a lot of people didn't seem to think it should take. The decisions all made perfect sense from my end. When I began studying medicine way back in high school, nearly everyone was supportive. I can't tell you specifically how I came to that decision though. It just "felt right".

Reminiscent to how I "felt disappointment" as a child with no good explanation. Prior to acceptance into medical school, you're required to write essays and put into words why you want to be a doctor. I found the words as best I could, but that's all they were – words. They do their best to describe the thing, however, they'll never actually be the thing.

As I was nearing the end of medical school though, for some reason, the path I was on started to "feel wrong". Similar to how there was no really good explanation why the opposite was true, and it "felt right" 10 years earlier, or why I "felt disappointment" as a child 10 years before that. But now there was no support.

I didn't understand. I hadn't hurt anyone. No crimes were committed. I went into medicine to study medicine. No one paid my way. What happened? I couldn't tell you specifically what changed in me, other than a "feeling". Everybody was lined up though, ready to tell me exactly why I made the decision I did. They wanted to pretend they knew.

It was because I was "flaky" or "irresponsible" or "immature" or insert whatever insult you'd like here _____. How did these people know this stuff? Did they really know me better than I knew myself? I presumed myself to be somewhat smart after scoring in the 99% percentile on my medical boards, but these people were obviously so much smarter than me.

I didn't even have the slightest clue to begin explaining how that "decision" came to me. However, these people knew beyond a shadow of a doubt what happened and why I was doing what I was doing (I put the word decision in quotes because, as I said, this felt more like direction or guidance from somewhere rather than a decision).

Not to belabor the point, but this type of situation is hard enough to deal with once. When it gets repeated over and over, decade after decade, it really starts to wear on you. Which is exactly what happened when I moved on from medicine to poker. And then from poker to screenwriting. Then again from screenwriting to golf. So there's your answer about the origins of my "crushing disappointment" and "desperate searches".

The only logical reason I can think of for receiving so such much blowback after every major decision in my life, is it has to do with one thing and one thing only. Money. This was the one common theme throughout all this. I've never put money as the number one reason for doing anything. Unfortunately, this tends to agitate and upset a very large segment of the population. That's how they control people. If you can't be controlled, the people with the gold are not going to be happy.

This is when the words like flaky, and irresponsible, and immature start getting dragged out. You're doing what you want to do, not what they want you to do. "Hey guys, this one's broke. It's got a mind of its own. I can't get it to do what I want." This absolutely terrifies them. Almost all power structures in the world operate off the principle of fear. If you won't cower before them, you're of no use to them.

What I find strange is, I've always thought, maybe naively, money would be fairly easy to come by for a person with above-average intelligence if they put their mind to it and made it their top priority. As I've said though, it never seemed a worthy goal, so I've never attempted it. I freely admit this is something I could be very wrong about, but I'll let someone else carry out that experiment.

Cat on a Hot Tin Roof

Since nobody seemed interested in answers other than "I'm in charge and said so", I decided to go out and find real ones. Take the bull by the horns and figure it out on my own. So, how did I do it? Good question.

How I did this is going to sound extremely bizarre. The whole thing is already ridiculously bizarre, but to help put this next section into some context and try to provide a little further evidence my motivation for writing this book is not solely money, I need to tell you a story or a joke. In the field of medicine, every specialty tends to get stereotyped as to the nature of the personalities that get attracted to them. Then people like to poke fun at each other for those traits.

For instance, emergency room doctors get called "the cowboys" of medicine, anesthesiologists are the "lazy bums", neurosurgeons are the "egomaniacs", and the comparisons go on and on. Well, if you remember what I said in the introduction about training in orthopedics, the joke about them goes, "How do you hide something from an orthopedic surgeon? You put it in a book". Implying they don't read so much or so good, take your pick, or both.

So, getting someone who was nearly an orthopedist to sit down and write a book could be probably be classified as a minor miracle of sorts. However, I believe the benefits of taking on such a monumental task (for someone like me) to be manifold. Not only has it given me a far greater appreciation for writers and what they do, I hope it also indicates how important I think this information is. After completing this project, let me tell you, there are much, much easier ways to make money.

That was also my long and roundabout way of trying to say - I've always been more of a movie guy than a book guy. Something you might have already noticed with the dropping of a Flatliners reference within the first five pages.

There's no shame in it. I don't dislike books. It just has to be a topic I'm really into. And it's always been that way for me going back to childhood. My sister was the book person. Big time. She read everything. Won all the contests at school. Couldn't find her without one. We were just different personalities. For my money, it was Indiana Jones, Star Wars, and Back to the Future.

Now, with that out of the way, we can finally get into it. The only other thing I wanted to mention is, I've always had surprisingly good intuition for someone teased with the labels of "dumb jock" or "mechanic". That's probably one of the reasons I excelled at poker with being able to read people and their intentions better than most. That word – intuition – covers a lot, and we'll go into some detail in chapter 3. I just wanted to bring it up here because it plays a crucial role in how this whole thing started.

Actually, there is one more thing I wanted to address before going on. I realize I may have lost a few readers with some of the outrageous claims made, and may lose a few more when the rest are recounted, and that's fine. I've also most likely damaged my professional reputation quite a bit with talking about this stuff, and that's fine as well.

My reason for being totally comfortable with all this has to do with the "life review" that accompanied my NDE. The life review I underwent was another very strange aspect that differed from the textbook cases, and I'll get into that later. However, the big take away from that process, for me, was that none of this stuff is private anyways.

That's a topic I'd struggled with and debated and argued about my entire life. What's private and what's public? Is there anything in this life we actually "own"? That's ours and ours alone? When working in a research hospital after graduating med school, I remember a colleague telling me in a matter of fact way, with no doubt in her mind, "There's no such thing as privacy".

She was absolutely certain and convinced there was no alternative. I was literally speechless. I wanted to rebut her claims and tell her, "Of course there's privacy", but for some inexplicable reason I remained silent. I pondered what she said for a while, but my final verdict ended up being no verdict because I didn't have enough evidence either way. I would revisit the issue every few years, yet there was no progress to be found.

I can say now, after what I've been through, I 100% agree with her. Our thoughts are real things. They have an existence apart from us and affect the world around us in dramatic ways - even if we do not voice them aloud.

There is no privacy, even in our own minds. This is just my experience however, and I'm aware it would be difficult to near impossible to convince anyone else of this. So, with that said, I will get on with my story knowing you are not the first audience to hear it.

Fire Walk with Me

Let's go back to the warm spring air of March, and the busted brackets of basketball tournaments. My aforementioned intuition was running at high levels. The blood, sweat and tears of the previous 5 years had been forged into refining my golf game to the point where I could make money from it professionally.

This had all fallen apart though, when a relative who promised to help fund the venture was now claiming he didn't remember anything of the sort. I was at one of those crises points talked about earlier.

They say most people switch careers an average of 5 times over the course of their lives. Not just different jobs within the same field, but entirely different career paths. Well, here I was, already working to find a 5th, years ahead of my 40th birthday.

One of the other nicknames I earned growing up besides "bandit", had been "clutch". This was given to me by a youth football coach who loved my uncanny ability to pick up a first down or make a score when we really needed it. Somehow those traits were surfacing here again, and a new path for my life was opening amidst the heartbreak and devastation of the golf disaster.

Like with the feelings I had about medicine being "right" or "wrong" at certain points in my life, this new path appearing before me didn't seem to have a good explanation. It just "happened". Comparable to how when playing football, big plays would just "happen".

Now, being trained as a scientist and overall a very curious person, I became interested in examining the behind the scenes workings of these events. There was a definite pattern here, but what exactly was happening? What were these feelings or abilities? Was this something I could control or influence?

Naturally, this lead to experimentation. Information and things seemed to come to me when I needed them. I had a passive (or so it appeared – we'll get into the unconscious more in chapter 3) relationship with whatever was going on. Was it possible for me to actively go and out and find what I wanted?

In passing several years earlier, I had come across the concept of remote viewing. The government spent over 20 million dollars on this program from the 1970's until it was cancelled in the mid 1990's. That is an enormous amount of time and money to invest in something that doesn't work. So, I began wondering if remote viewing was something I could do as well?

Sure enough, it was. Similar to how I made an unconscious "target" of where my life path would go after retiring from golf, I could also make a "target" of any object or person or thing, and then go find it. Nobody formally trained me to do this. Everybody's method will be unique and different, but for me, the best way I can describe it is like "surfing".

The information was out there like an ocean of data, and it was only a matter of looking around until finding the answer to a question. This was all happening in the mind. However, there was still something about it that didn't quite satisfy me. It was still too passive.

It continued to feel like the information was coming to me instead of going out and getting it. So, I designed another experiment. The information I was surfing had to be coming from somewhere. There was a "place" it originated from before getting to me. I needed to go to that place.

If this hasn't been weird enough for you already, this is where it starts getting super weird. My logic may breakdown in your opinion, but once you've successfully remote viewed, it's sort of like cracking open an egg on what you think is possible.

This "place" with the information existed. I'd surfed the waves emanating from there with my mind. Now, I just needed to physically go there. The questions then became, "Where exactly is this place and how do I get there?"

And that's why I brought up movies earlier. I went through a lot of schooling. More than 20 years of sitting in classrooms. No one ever brought up different dimensions that I recall. "String" theory with its curled up dimensions had crossed my path, but they also make sure to emphasize how it's all theoretical. The only other discussion I'd seen of different dimensions was the movies.

I mentally started reviewing all the movies I'd seen, searching for clues that might help. By chance, I remembered the somewhat recent movie Jumper with Hayden Christensen (the actor who played Anakin Skywalker in the Star Wars Prequels). In it, he can teleport through time and space and go wherever he wants – ancient Egypt, Rome, bank vaults, etc.

That got my wheels spinning, and I thought, "You know what? Not such a bad idea to get to the place where the information is coming from. I'll just jump there." There was no device or technology allowing him to do this in the movie, he just somehow did it with his mind – similar to what I'd been doing with remote viewing.

Out of the Frying Pan

After dinner that night, I was relaxing in bed thinking through the specifics of how to perform this jump. All I knew was - I had to make a jump using only my mind.

Well, what did I know about jumping in the physical world? There's a starting point and a destination. The destination was clear – the information dimension. I just needed somewhere to begin. When I thought back to the movie Jumper, I remembered he would take off from his living room among other places. The more I thought about it, what he seemed to be doing was teleporting rather than jumping.

That led to searching my memory banks for other movies involving travel to different dimensions. What else did I know about jumping in the physical world? It always involved a change in elevation. Were there any movies about jumping from heights and visits to strange lands?

The movie The Matrix then surfaced into my awareness. Specifically, the scene where Neo is put through a "jump program" and attempts an impossible leap from one skyscraper to another. This could be promising. Not only was Neo in a strange land, but also in a strange state of mind. Both of those were things I was after.

I closed my eyes and began constructing a visualization of the jump program scene, but with myself as the main character instead of Neo. I mentally put myself on top of the building and tried to remember the advice imparted by his mentors. The snippets of dialogue that came back were not encouraging.

One of the characters remarks, "No one ever makes their first jump." OK, not what I needed to hear. Another warns, "If you die in the program, you also die in real life." This sounded like some Freddy Krueger nonsense of The Nightmare on Elm Street fame. I'd never been hurt in my dreams before. Then again, I never imagined I'd have been remote viewing a few days earlier.

In summary, all signs pointed to a lot of pain. No one makes their first jump, and when you inevitably miss, it's going to hurt badly. Unless of course you're The One. Nothing in my life up to this point though, would indicate that to be the case.

I weighed these conclusions against the disappointment and desperation haunting me since childhood, and calculated there was not a whole lot to lose. So, in my visualization, I took a running start just like Neo in The Matrix, and jumped as far as I could.

Well, I guess I wasn't The One. I was still in bed and there was no new dimension to be found. But, something did happen. For a brief moment after takeoff, there was a feeling of freeness. Similar to how you might feel on the big drop of a roller coaster, or I would imagine sky diving, although I've never done that.

A feeling where you slightly lose connection with your body. It's something I'd also experienced a few times playing basketball, when going up for a shot or trying to block one. Somehow, that feeling could be achieved without the mechanical aid of an amusement park or the physical body when playing sports. This had been done purely with the mind.

So, I did not cross the chasm between the buildings. Or, relocate to the dimension with the information. However, I had also not fallen multiple stories to the pavement and injured myself. Something had changed for a brief moment. And I was pretty much unscathed outside of damage to my ego for thinking I might be The One. More experimentation was definitely in order.

I needed to find a way to prolong or amplify that feeling of freeness. I went back to the skyscrapers and jump program looking for improvements, but something was not quite right.

The problem turned out to be, I was putting myself into a scene from a movie conjured by another person's imagination. I was only controlling one character in a world that belonged to someone else. I needed a new movie. One that could help me construct a more individual visualization.

What were my choices of movies featuring jumping in a way I could relate to on a personal level? For this, my memory returned with the documentary movie titled The Bridge, which tells the history of the Golden Gate Bridge in San Francisco, California and the story of "jumpers" and their attraction to it.

San Francisco was familiar to me. When playing poker after med school, I lived in a small studio apartment adjacent to Golden Gate Park. I also visited the Bay Area as part of a family vacation as a youth. Creating a strong visualization of the bridge was not going to be a problem. Best of all, they were entirely images from my own memory. It seemed a perfect fit. I began constructing the world in my mind, and instead of placing myself on a skyscraper from The Matrix, I was now standing on the Golden Gate Bridge.

This was the key to success. I was no longer in a dry, cold computer simulation, but surrounded with rich sensory input. The feel and sound of the biting winds trying to knock me off balance were tangible. Noises from passing automobiles and the conversations of pedestrian traffic crossing the bridge were astoundingly lifelike. Looking down at the water, I could even feel the sense of space and distance to the water as well as the sounds from the ocean itself.

Here's what I was getting at when I brought up being scared and having courage earlier. I was more standing on the bridge at this point than lying in bed. This felt more real than wherever my body was. Maybe they were right when they said, "If you die here, you die in real life". Now I was scared.

There was still an awareness of my body at this point. It's just my attention was focused more on being on the bridge than lying in bed. If you pressed me to be scientific and put numbers on it, I can't give a specific number like 90% or 75%, but it was definitely more than half. And well, I was there. Or, there I was. That's where I wanted to be. Could I do what I went there to do?

Only one way to find out for sure whether people are right about stuff and that's to experience it yourself. The movies said I could really die, but in my mind there wasn't a whole lot I was fond of in the world. So, I gathered my courage, calmed my fears, steadied myself, and jumped.

Turns out I was wrong. There must have been things I was still attached to. About 20% of the way down I was forced to abort and pull out of the imagery because it was too intense. Similar to how the feel of the wind and sounds of the ocean were remarkably real, the feelings of fear and panic and regret were also just as real. I pondered the situation and tried to determine what was holding me back.

Was there really anything for me in this world, or was I just afraid? Honest analysis revealed fear. So, I set about the hard work of recreating the visualization, determined to win the battle with myself.

The second attempt was just as nerve wracking as the first. Even though I convinced myself intellectually it didn't matter, there were still the feelings that go along with knowing it's going to happen. As I traveled faster and farther from the bridge though, a sense of peace slowly came over me. After a certain point, there was an inevitability about it and nothing I could do would change the result.

Or, so I thought. My life had taken so many surprising turns recently, when the inevitable didn't turn out to be the inevitable, it didn't come as much of a shocker. The last few feet before hitting the water there was a sudden burst of light. What happened next, I can only describe as getting "ejected" out of not only my visualization, but also of my physical body.

Rising from the Ashes

In the blink of an eye, I went from falling incredibly fast towards the water beneath the Golden Gate Bridge, to floating leisurely above an unrecognizable new reality. Before I get into any specific observations of this surreal environment, it's important to take note of the speed aspect here, both before and after the transition, because it's going to come up again later when we try to understand what happened. The reentry phase will also be another particularly important place to pay attention.

At first, what stood out most was the abruptness of the change between the two worlds. There was no smoothness or gradualness. No fade in or out. Dissolve into or jump cut/smash edit. Even if I used the analogy of switching from watching one movie to a completely different one, it wouldn't do it justice.

It was more along the lines of going from watching a movie to getting attacked by a shark. Only you're not even sure if it's a shark, it's just this thing your mind has to deal with right here and right now. A shark attack is not a good description either, other than conveying the abundance of conflicting emotions and thoughts one might experience in that type of situation. However, this was not a new situation or even a new place I was thrust into, it seemed to be an entirely new existence.

The shark attack analogy also fails to capture the essence because it implies things like fear and violence, which highlights the second thing that stood out most - an overwhelming sense of peace and well-being. There was a complete absence of pain and suffering. Worry didn't seem to exist. I was not worried about my body or how I would get back to it.

These are only concerns when reflecting back, "What if this? Or, what if that happened?" In that state, I got the impression I could easily have gone on to do other things without looking back. This is why I encourage people not to attempt this. If there's no worries about returning, then you may not. There could be mechanisms at work allowing people to go where they need without worry or fear, but I can't tell you that for sure. I'm going to stick with being lucky as an explanation.

Those were my initial feelings on entry to this new realm. The thoughts were similar to the feelings and embodied that "freeing" sensation I described earlier you sometimes get on the big drop of a rollercoaster, only in the most extreme form you can imagine.

So, while there was freedom from pain and suffering, there was also a freedom and expansion of thought. The level of understanding and awareness seemed increased. That little voice in your head that's always second guessing, doubting yourself and others, and constantly reexamining from different angles wasn't there anymore. Things just kind of were, but they also made sense. There was no thinking required to understand, because somehow you already knew stuff.

We've covered how I felt and thought. Now, I guess I should give a little description of the place itself. This is going to be incredibly difficult for several reasons. In the ordinary world our senses betray us all the time. Whether optical illusions or just trying to keep our balance walking down the street.

We're intimately familiar with our 5 physical senses, using them day after day, year after year, yet they still manage to get the best of us. So, trying to describe what I "saw" in a place where "eyes" don't exist is going to be a near impossible task. Coupled with the fact I wasn't there very long, with no opportunity to learn any complex tasks equivalent to riding a bicycle, it gets even harder.

Finally, as mentioned, awareness was increased, so while this will be a linear account, many of these things came into my thoughts simultaneously. Some NDEs have described it as having 360-degree "vision".

With that in mind, the following is what I "saw" and how it played out. And what I "saw" could easily have been images generated by the subconscious mind or some deeper aspect of consciousness. I firmly believe, and will present evidence for later, what took place here was my consciousness (either whole or part) having an experience while separated from my physical brain.

The first part, which I already alluded to, involved going from a head first position and approaching the water at high velocity, to then being oriented upright and floating above a new world after passing through some kind of transition involving a flash of light.

From there, I was moving in a "forward" direction the whole time at a little faster than leisurely pace and neither the speed nor the destination seemed under my conscious control. There was no "sound" or not much of it. There could have been the sound of a light breeze or air going by, but no music or trumpets. The image below me was that of a valley or canyon, but it did not seem to have a 3 dimensional quality to it. Like I could crash into it and not hurt myself.

It's also possible it was I who lacked the substance, because there appeared to be wisps of things floating in the canyon. Their precise shape was hard to make out due to the distance. They were spread out from each other and numbered a couple dozen or so. I guessed they were beings similar to me, since I did not feel like I had a body. It may also be that the valley had the same wispy quality as well. My focus quickly went from what was below me to the direction I was traveling.

The sky was painted with brilliant colors. Not a sunset, but the colors you might find in one. There was no water anywhere, however I looked to see if I could spot the bridge I jumped from. It was no longer there, but rather than confusion I remember feeling amusement or wonder or astonishment or even all of that together. I turned my attention back in the forward direction and there were two wispy beings in the distance I was approaching.

They were closer together than the ones in the valley and my path seemed to be heading slightly above them. I was positioned between them, but more toward the one on the right. As I got closer, their shapes became clearer and the closest description I can provide is of large wispy whitish semi-transparent flying stingrays with pronounced wings. And even though they were wispy and semi-transparent they also had a luminous or glowing quality to them.

After almost completely passing over the top of them, the strangest thing so far occurred. I began getting pulled towards the flying being on the right and below me. This was upsetting because I was having a good time and didn't appreciate the interruption. The pulling didn't seem to be occurring in a straight line either. More in the fashion of how things circle a drain. Or maybe a spiral vortex or orbit.

The speed I was traveling at also increased with this pulling sensation. It was almost a feeling of being suddenly captured against my will. The next thing I knew; I was back in the physical world. Not only was I back in my body, something else was there too. Or someone else would be a more accurate.

I was struggling to breathe and didn't understand why. It felt like I was working extra hard to do the breathing of what a 300 lb. man might have to do (while also having to do my own breathing).

It felt like I could "let go" of this other more difficult breathing pattern if I wanted, and be left with my own, but I was extremely curious about what was going on. So, I fought to "hang on" to both patterns until I could figure out what was happening. Then it hit me. There was a familiar quality to this second breathing pattern. It was someone I knew. The 300 lb. man was my father in the room next door.

Some decisions had to be made now. I had adjusted well and gained control of both patterns without too much difficulty. The scientist in me was bursting with joy in anticipation of possible experiments to be conducted.

For the next several minutes I debated the ethics of this once in a lifetime opportunity. However, the novelty of the situation had finally worn off a bit and leaving quietly appeared to be the only right option, since I wouldn't want tests run on me without consent. Somewhat grudgingly, I abandoned both bodies and settled back into my own.

END

A Brief Epilogue

First, I want to say thank you to the fans of this work who made this book possible.

For those interested in what I'll be doing next. It does seem like my life has hit that Second Act area I talked about in my dramatic discussion and the problems/adventures appear to be increasing in intensity.

There is some new content already available on my website since the publishing of this book that may be included in the next volume of work. I can't say for certain what will happen, but as part of the increasing intensity mentioned I would expect to see more physical expression in the world.

There will most likely be surprises along the way. Big and small. I don't want to get into the details. However, there most certainly will be some fun or I won't be involved.

So, with that said, thank you again.

About the Author

Jason Nealon graduated Magna Cum Laude with a major in Biology and a minor in Chemistry and was a member of the prestigious Phi Beta Kappa National Honor Society at the University of South Carolina in Columbia, SC. While there, he was also selected as a special research fellow for work on the Human Genome Project in collaboration with the National Institutes of Health, South Carolina Cancer Center and the University of South Carolina School of Medicine.

Jason received his medical degree from the University of Miami Miller School of Medicine in Miami, FL. His focus there was in the area of Orthopedic Surgery and excelled once again academically scoring in the 99th percentile on the National Board of Medical Examiners Licensing Exam. Although granted interviews at the top Orthopedic programs in the country, such as the NYU Hospital for Joint Diseases, he chose to forego surgical residency training at that time.

www.ingramcontent.com/pod-product-compliance
Lightning Source LLC
LaVergne TN
LVHW051620080426
835511LV00016B/2082